STEPPING into DRAMA

A Midsummer Night's Dream in the Elementary Classroom

GEORGE BELLIVEAU

STEPPING into DRAMA

A Midsummer Night's Dream in the Elementary Classroom

PACIFIC EDUCATIONAL PRESS
Vancouver, Canada

Stepping into Drama: *A Midsummer Night's Dream* in the Elementary Classroom
Copyright © George Belliveau 2014
ISBN: 978-1-926966-70-0

Published by Pacific Educational Press
Faculty of Education
University of British Columbia
411 – 2389 Health Sciences Mall
Vancouver, BC V6T 1Z3

Telephone: 604-822-5385
Fax: 604-822-6603
Email: pep.admin@ubc.ca
Website: www.pacificedpress.ca

All rights reserved. Pacific Educational Press is a member of Access Copyright. Purchasers of this resource have permission to reproduce materials in Appendices A to H. No other part of this publication may be reproduced, stored in a retrieval system, or transmitted in any form or by any means, electronic, mechanical, photocopying, recording, or otherwise without the prior written permission of the publisher or a licence from Access Copyright. For a copyright licence, visit accesscopyright.ca or call toll-free 1-800-893-5777.

The 30-minute adapted play script of *A Midsummer Night's Dream* that is included in this book is also available as class sets for student use (ISBN 978-1-926966-71-7). Contact pep.sales@ubc.ca for ordering information or visit the publisher's website (www.pacificedpress.ca).

We acknowledge the financial support of the Government of Canada through the Canada Book Fund (CBF) for our publishing activities.

Library and Archives Canada Cataloguing in Publication

Belliveau, George André, 1968-, author
Stepping into drama : a Midsummer night's dream in the elementary classroom / George Belliveau.

Includes bibliographical references and index.
Issued in print and electronic formats.
ISBN 978-1-926966-70-0 (pbk.). —ISBN 978-1-926966-72-4 (epub). —
ISBN 978-1-926966-73-1 (mobi)

1. Shakespeare, William,—1564-1616—Study and teaching (Elementary).
2. English drama—Study and teaching (Elementary). 3. Shakespeare, William, 1564-1616. Midsummer night's dream. 4. Drama in education.
I. Title. II. Title: Midsummer night's dream in the elementary classroom.

PR2987.B44 2014   372.66'044   C2014-901658-1   C2014-901659-X

Cover photographs: top right: © David Sims; centre left and right: © Sue Belliveau; bottom right: © Barbara Kuhne.
Interior photographs: pages 16, 26, 49, 54, 55, 62, 112, 114, 117, 126 © Sue Belliveau; page 56 © Barbara Kuhne; pages 104, 110 © David Sims; page 70 © Graham Lea; pages 103 and 124, Wikimedia Commons (public domain)

Design and layout: Mauve Pagé, pageanddesign.com
Editing: Laura Edlund and Barbara Kuhne
Proofreading: Nancy Wilson
Indexing: Stephen Ullstrom

Printed in Canada
17 16 15 14 — 1 2 3 4

MIX
Paper from responsible sources
FSC® C004071

For Sue, Maddie, and Sophie.

 **CONTENTS**

ACKNOWLEDGEMENTS · 9

INTRODUCTION · 11
Why Shakespeare for Young Learners? · 11
What Does This Book Offer? · 12
Overview: How to Use This Book · 13

PART I: RESEARCH, CURRICULUM LINKS, ASSESSMENT, PLANNING, AND ADDITIONAL RESOURCES · 17
Research · 18
Curriculum Links · 19
Assessment · 20
Planning · 21
Additional Resources and References · 23

PART II: DISCOVERING SHAKESPEARE AND *A MIDSUMMER NIGHT'S DREAM* · 27
Role Dramas · 28
Using the Role Dramas · 30
Role Drama 1: Who Art Thou Shakespeare? · 31
Role Drama 2: Athenian Market · 40
Role Drama 3: Character Masks · 47

PART III: ENGAGING WITH THE STORY OF *A MIDSUMMER NIGHT'S DREAM* · 57

Using the Story Version and Lessons · 58
Lesson 1: Mighty Law of Athens and Runaway Plan · 60
Lesson 2: A Play for Theseus' Wedding Day · 66
Lesson 3: Titania and Oberon Clash · 71
Lesson 4: Spells Are Everywhere in the Wood · 76
Lesson 5: Puck Plays in Devilish Ways · 81
Lesson 6: Lovers' Quarrel · 87
Lesson 7: Release of Spells and All Is Well · 92
Lesson 8: Play Within the Play on the Wedding Day · 97

PART IV: FROM PAGE TO STAGE: SHARING THE PLAY ADAPTATION · 105

Production Considerations · 107
Rehearsal Considerations · 114

PART V: ADAPTED SCRIPT: *A MIDSUMMER NIGHT'S DREAM* · 127

APPENDICES

Appendix A: Glossary of Drama Games and Strategies · 181
Appendix B: Materials for Role Drama 1: Who Art Thou Shakespeare? · 188
Appendix C: Materials for Role Drama 2: Athenian Market · 194
Appendix D: Materials for Role Drama 3: Character Masks · 199
Appendix E: *Dream*: A Story Version · 204
Appendix F: Materials for Lesson 7: Young Athenians' Journey · 209
Appendix G: Materials for Lesson 8: Hearing the Text Activity · 211
Appendix H: Materials for Rehearsal Considerations: Character Journal · 213

REFERENCES · 215

INDEX · 221

ACKNOWLEDGEMENTS

THERE ARE A NUMBER OF PEOPLE I WOULD LIKE TO ACKNOWLEDGE and thank, as without them the book would not be what it is. First, I wish to sincerely thank the children, parents, teachers, and administration from the school research site. Their willingness to participate and offer feedback made possible the five-year project on building community through drama and Shakespeare. I wish to acknowledge funding support from the Social Sciences and Humanities Research Council, and the University of British Columbia (Humanities and Social Sciences grant, Faculty of Education, and the Department of Language and Literacy Education). Thank you to Jaime Beck, David Beare, Mindy Carter, Ray Doiron, Shelley Hymel, Carl Leggo, Donnard MacKenzie, Laurie Murphy, Monica Prendergast, Kathryn Ricketts, Ahava Shira, Amanda Wager, Vincent White, Sarah Wolfman-Robichaud, and Eva Ziltener, who contributed to this project in various ways. I wish to acknowledge my colleague and friend, Lynn Fels, who helped describe a number of the drama strategies included in this book and introduced me to role drama. Graham W. Lea co-conceived and co-developed an earlier version of the Athenian Market role drama and provided valuable feedback throughout this project—thank you.

Thank you to Catherine Edwards for welcoming and supporting this project from day one. Barbara Kuhne was equally supportive and guided this project with openness, grace, and trust. Thank you to Laura Edlund for her excellent editorial suggestions. It is a privilege to work with such experienced editors. Thank you also to Mauve Pagé for the book design and to the Pacific Educational Press team (including Kaye Banez, Natalia Cornwall, Clare Quirico, Nancy Wilson, and Sharlene Eugenio), who brought their expertise to producing this book. Thank you to Richard

Carter, whom I respect and admire for the remarkable work he does with children in his Community and Shakespeare Company.

A special acknowledgement to my wife, Sue Belliveau, for inspiring me to write this book. Her years of creatively integrating drama in her elementary classroom, and in particular Shakespeare, exemplify her genuine belief in fostering children's imagination and potential. The ideas in this book owe much to her artistic pedagogy. Thank you, Sue, and many other inspirational teachers, for the daily work you do with children. I also wish to acknowledge my parents for their continuous support. Last but not least, thank you to Maddie and Sophie, my beautiful daughters, who have endured listening to their parents talk endlessly about Shakespeare.

NOTE: To abide by university and school board ethical policies, names of teachers, students, parents, and researchers are not identified in the book. Oral and written feedback came primarily from six teachers, twelve parents, over one hundred 6–12 year olds, and three researchers/observers, all of whom gave consent to share their comments, illustrations, and photos.

INTRODUCTION

WHY SHAKESPEARE FOR YOUNG LEARNERS?

> If I had to choose one reason why Shakespeare was valuable for my [7-year-old] daughter ... I think I would say ... the *worldliness* she gained by learning Shakespeare. Why learn about Columbus? Why learn about the Black Plague? Why know a Beatles song when you hear it? You should just know these things, because even if you don't care about them directly, they affect the world around you. —PARENT

THIS BOOK PRESENTS A SEQUENCE OF DRAMA-BASED STRATEGIES FOR introducing Shakespeare in the elementary grades (ages 6–12). The teacher-friendly approaches are based on the work of experienced elementary teachers in Vancouver, Canada, who have been exploring Shakespeare with children for over a decade. These interactive strategies complement the work at the Royal Shakespeare Company (RSC), where researchers and practitioners introduce Shakespeare to young learners (Winston and Tandy 2012). The RSC group has found that Shakespeare should be taught as early as possible because children four or five years old are more "fearless" and "they are used to trying out new language" (Curtis 2008). Likewise, our experience in Vancouver has been that young children working with Shakespeare become highly engaged with the rich and playful language, stories, and complex characters. This engagement with Shakespeare at an early age exposes students to a "worldliness," a cultural literacy to be built upon throughout their education and lives. Shakespeare's plays offer a bridge to discover and discuss some of the great questions in life.

WHAT DOES THIS BOOK OFFER?

The detailed lessons offered in this book are informed by classroom experiences and research, and explore pedagogical strategies that have been effective for introducing children to Shakespeare, and in particular to *A Midsummer Night's Dream* (referred to as *Dream*).

Over the last few decades a number of educators and scholars have contributed valuable ideas and pedagogical approaches to bringing Shakespeare to young learners. This book is unique in that it provides a series of detailed drama lessons to support your literacy program, along with age-appropriate production and rehearsal strategies to mount a Shakespearean play with your class.

Rather than introducing a number of different Shakespearean plays, this book centres on *Dream* and presents it both in story form and as an adapted script. The benefits of focusing on *one* play are that teachers can:

» follow a specific sequence of lessons on one piece of literature
» go deeper inside one particular story
» see direct and sustained links to their literacy curriculum
» help their students lift the words and characters off the page for a shared presentation within their school

Most activities in this book could be adapted for another play, or even applied to picture books, short stories, or other literary works. However, each activity has been carefully selected and developed for students and teachers exploring *Dream*.

Suitable for All Teachers

The ideas in this book are suitable for teachers with little or no previous experience with drama or Shakespeare as well as seasoned drama teachers looking for new ideas for their classrooms. Teachers new to drama might only select a few drama activities from the book to support their literacy and learning program. As they gradually build comfort and confidence, they might increase the amount of drama-based strategies to eventually integrate the full sequence of lessons described in this book. The detailed drama activities build one upon the other; however, many of them can be done individually and do not require the entire sequence. Part I suggests a plan for including a range of activities and integrating the continuum of suggestions in this book.

Suitable for All Students and Diverse Learners

The activities in the book are meant to be inclusive and are conceptualized with the understanding that classrooms are diverse learning environments. To meet various classroom needs, teachers should feel free to adapt and/or modify the lessons to suit their student population. It should be noted that most of the drama activities included in the book have been developed in classrooms where some students were identified as special needs and/or learning English as an additional language. A number of the non-verbal, visual, and kinesthetic activities have been shown to build confidence for different types of learners. As well, the repetition of the script work has proven to develop pronunciation and comprehension for diverse learners.

OVERVIEW: HOW TO USE THIS BOOK

This book combines the sequence of lesson plans, *Dream* story version, adapted script version of *Dream*, and other support so that teachers have all the resources they need in one book. As well, it offers links to curriculum objectives and assessment strategies, along with student, parent, researcher, and teacher reflections. The combination of practical classroom instruction and theoretical background offers teachers insights into *how* and *why* engaging young learners with Shakespeare can be a rich learning experience.

PART I shares some background literature on drama and literacy. This section highlights current research on Shakespeare and young learners. In addition, it includes a discussion about curriculum links and assessment, along with planning suggestions and a timeline to integrate and build on the ideas from this book.

PART II includes three role dramas to help students enter the world of Shakespeare and *Dream*. The role dramas are specifically designed to:

» provide context about the author and the play
» pique the curiosity and ignite the imagination of young learners through a sequence of user-friendly activities
» lead the children and teacher(s) to explore the world of Shakespeare's *Dream*, initially without an audience

The role dramas are self-contained, so that teachers can choose any one or more to use.

PART III offers eight lessons to use with an abridged story version of *Dream*, which is provided in Appendix E. The story of *Dream* is told in eight parts, which correspond to the eight lessons. Thus, the lessons are sequential. Each lesson includes the following:

» warm-up activities
» vocabulary development
» story-reading and drama-based activities
» drawing and writing options

These activities allow for exploration and experimentation with the story, characters, and language. The detailed lessons are supplemented by samples of visual and written work from students, along with comments from teachers and researcher/observer insights.

PART IV consists of suggestions and schedules for producing and staging an adapted version of the play, for which a script is given in Part V. This section provides:

» ways to engage young students with the Shakespearean text through rehearsal strategies
» practical production suggestions for teachers to consider as they move towards sharing the work with an audience

Note that the aim of this process is not necessarily to share a tightly rehearsed and polished production. Instead, the actual production can be an invitation to an audience to observe a magical world created by the young learners and to celebrate the children's work, regardless of what stage they are at when the production occurs. In other words, the goal is for students to fully engage every day with *Dream* and their class in diverse and challenging ways.

PART V presents an adapted 30-minute play script for teachers to use in their classrooms.

If teachers wish to stage a reading or production with their students, they are encouraged to acquire a class set of student scripts. The font size in the specially designed student script version is larger for easy reading. As well, the pride and ownership of students having their very own bound scripts increases their commitment

to literacy and the dramatic process. A photocopied script typically does not generate this type of excitement for children.

APPENDICES present materials to support the preceding portions of the book, including the following:

» glossary of drama activities and games, organized alphabetically for easy reference
» materials for the three role dramas in Part II, including reproducible pages
» materials to support Part III—the lessons that explore the story version of *Dream*
» the story version of *Dream*

Within Parts I to IV, references are made to the material in the Appendices. Terms in the glossary appear in **boldface** in Parts I to IV.

PART I

RESEARCH, CURRICULUM LINKS, ASSESSMENT, PLANNING, AND ADDITIONAL RESOURCES

RESEARCH

OVER THE LAST FOUR DECADES, RESEARCHERS HAVE EXPLORED AND documented how and why teachers can use the arts to benefit students in various ways. (A complete reference list appears at the back of the book.) Studying the integration and application of various art forms within and across the curriculum, researchers and practitioners have written extensively about the benefits of applying arts-based approaches in teaching (Catterall 2002; Deasy 2002; Hetland and Winner 2001; Winner, Goldstein, and Vincent-Lancrin 2013). Therefore, it is important for teachers to recognize that introducing drama and Shakespeare to children is an effective pedagogical approach supported by decades of research from scholars and practitioners. Studies on using drama with young learners point to benefits in various areas including the following:

» reading comprehension (Wagner and Barnett 1998)
» writing (Moore and Caldwell 1993)
» motivation (Deasy 2002)
» problem solving (Catterall 1998)
» empathy (Beare and Belliveau 2007; Kardash and Wright 1987)
» socio-emotional learning (Beare 2011)

Furthermore, the use of drama-based approaches in the classroom is supported by the work of literacy scholars who find that predicting and finding connections within a text increases students' ability and willingness to read and comprehend (Baldwin and Fleming 2003; Booth 2005; Smith and Herring 2001; Wilhelm 2002). Drama-based activities invite students to imagine the world of the literature, offering entry points and building confidence while engaging with the literary work (Bowell and Heap 2001). Researchers have shown how drama becomes a critical way to explore various content areas of the curriculum (Fels and Belliveau 2008).

As well, there is convincing evidence that using drama-based pedagogical strategies is an effective way to build integrated and engaging curricula in language arts classrooms and beyond (Anderson 2012). The practical strategies shared throughout this text are informed by recent scholarship into how drama builds understanding, expands curricular knowledge, and activates learning (Anderson and Dunn 2013; O'Connor 2010).

This book is also supported by the author's extensive five-year investigation of the effects of engaging in process drama strategies and staging adapted versions of Shakespearean plays with elementary students (Belliveau 2008–12, Social Sciences and Humanities Research Council Research Grant). This research project gathered data from four multigrade classrooms of elementary students, their teachers, family members, and other members of the school community. The findings of this research project complement those of earlier studies, suggesting that a drama-based integrated curricular process has positive effects for students in comprehension, writing, speaking, socio-emotional learning, arts appreciation, motivation, and artistic development (Belliveau 2009, 2012; Shira and Belliveau 2012; MacKenzie, Belliveau, Beck, Lea, and Wager 2011).

CURRICULUM LINKS

Engaging in drama activities and play production responds to a number of curricular goals in literacy, language arts, social studies, and social responsibility. The drama lessons in Parts II and III include curriculum links for teachers to consider while introducing the various strategies to students. These links cut across a number of subject areas, but most often support curricular objectives for language arts, social studies, and the expressive arts.

The drama lessons in Parts II and III are designed to foster and develop both critical and creative thinking. The majority of drama strategies involve problem solving: sustained concentration is required and decisions need to be made, individually or in groups. Role-playing often asks students to interpret, analyze, and present their work, prompting children to make purposeful choices in their creative work. As such, children are developing critical thinking skills and a variety of communication strategies, along with their artistic skills.

The drama-based activities in this book provide opportunities for students to interpret characters, ideas, and feelings drawn from the fictional world of *Dream*. Role-playing involves an act of imagination that is of central importance in developing the ability to understand others and build empathy. As students "live through" experiences of others, they learn to understand a variety of points of view and motives, and to empathize with others, thus building their socio-emotional capacity.

They also learn to clarify their own point of view and develop their ability to think carefully. By working in real and imagined worlds, students become better listeners, speakers, questioners, and creators. **Debriefing circles** at the end of each lesson allow students to explore personal connections and experiences by sharing their views, listening to others, and then writing about their experiences. Engaging in drama-based work enables students to practise negotiating, become more spontaneous, and develop inter- and intra-personal skills.

> Three times per year we are expected to do reading assessments with our class. I am convinced that the fluidity, attention to punctuation, [and] enunciation ... which some of my students have been able to exhibit during these assessments are directly related to the work on the play. There's also a confidence to read that really happens at the end of the year, once we've been doing Shakespeare for a few months. —TEACHER

ASSESSMENT

Throughout the drama lessons, teacher observation notes and oral feedback to students are critical as they provide benchmarks for both teachers and students during the process. Teachers can use a checklist to document specific goals or skills they wish their students to demonstrate during the activities. As well, a number of assessment strategies are suggested for specific activities.

- » In Part II, you will find suggestions for assessing student progress and offering feedback in conjunction with the role dramas.
- » In Part III, the journal writing and drawing represent an opportunity for teachers to respond to student learning and output, thus enabling teachers to assess areas where they might need to provide more support for particular students.
- » In Part IV, suggestions for a number of tasks (such as character journals, a play program, a newspaper, and a final written reflection) offer opportunities for assessment as well. These writing tasks give students the chance to show their understanding and their ability to present their knowledge in creative, written, visual, and oral forms. After the production, the final assignment entails students writing a letter to a friend or family member who could not see the play. This offers an opportunity for students to describe key events and synthesize the play, the production, and their learning.

PLANNING

It is important to think of the activities in this book as offering a continuum *and* a range that can be adapted to the time and resources available, students' level of experience and their interests, and teachers' comfort and confidence levels.

INITIAL MONTHS:	LEADING TOWARDS:	LEADING TOWARDS:	LAYING THE FOUNDATION FOR:
gradually introduce drama games and activities, such as those presented in Appendix A	more sustained role-playing in Part II	a closer look at the story, characters, and language of *Dream* in Part III through a story version	students rehearsing and producing an adapted play version of *Dream* in Parts IV and V

Note that it is not productive to compare the dramatic work you do in your classroom with the standards of professional, fully equipped theatres. Your purpose should focus on pedagogy and community building, taking the work forward with these priorities in mind. This is not to deny or discard aesthetics and creativity. On the contrary, encourage and nurture your students' artistic capabilities, but this is not the primary goal. The joy of creating and "playing" with Shakespeare and drama should always be front and centre.

Other considerations are time and level of completion. You may find, like the teacher quoted below, that you run out of rehearsal time for the dramatic presentation outlined in Part IV. Remember, however, the goal of performing *Dream* is not to present a polished, perfected piece but instead to share what you have explored with others so they can witness part of your class journey. This may mean modifying your goals, for example, and only sharing part of the play or some of the process with the audience.

> A few years ago, we were doing *The Tempest* in my grade 1–3 class, and as the production date approached, we realized we hadn't rehearsed Act 5 nearly enough. It wasn't ready to share. So, we had a class meeting where we decided that our Act 5 would be a physical re-enactment of the events with two narrators. Using two of my stronger grade 3 readers, we created a narrative version of *The Tempest*'s Act 5, where students "physicalized" the narration read by their peers and developed tableaux to depict the story. I think most parents thought this was planned as the story of the play simply continued; we just used a different performing style for Act 5, one we had used while reading the story version of the play. —TEACHER

Year-long Sample Calendar

SEPTEMBER

		1hr		
		1hr		
		1hr		
		1hr		

1 hour per week

OCTOBER

		1hr		
		1hr		
		1hr		
		1hr		

1 hour per week

NOVEMBER

	1hr		1hr	
	1hr		1hr	
	1hr		1hr	
	1hr		1hr	

2 hours per week

DECEMBER

1hr		1hr
1hr		1hr
1hr		1hr
1hr		1hr

2 hours per week

JANUARY

	1hr		1hr
	1hr		2hr
	1hr		1hr
	1hr		2hr

2–3 hours per week

FEBRUARY

1hr		1hr
1hr		2hr
1hr		1hr
1hr		2hr

2–3 hours per week

MARCH

1hr		1hr
1hr		2hr
1hr		1hr
1hr		2hr

2–3 hours per week

APRIL

2hr		2hr		2hr
2hr		3hr		2hr
2hr		3hr		2hr
2hr		3hr		2hr

6–8 hours per week

MAY

2hr		2hr		2hr
2hr		3hr		2hr
2hr		3hr		2hr
3hr		2hr		3hr

6–8 hours per week

JUNE

	3hr	3hr	3hr	
2hr	3hr	3hr	2hr	2hr
3hr	3hr	3hr	2hr	

9–12 hours per week

The year-long calendar above shows an example of a continuum with the gradual integration of drama into the classroom. The calendar is based on the typical 10-month (September to June) school year in North America.

» For the first four months, using drama games and activities once or twice per week for 45 minutes to an hour whenever possible helps students get accustomed to doing drama in the class. Activities can include improvisation, movement, **tableau**-work, and some concentration and trust-building group work.

» In months five through seven, you may extend the drama work towards more sustained lessons by using role drama, story drama, or short **play-building** projects for a special school event. (Part II suggests resources that complement the role dramas.)

> In months eight through ten, you may work towards rehearsing and producing a stage adaptation of *Dream*, as in Parts IV and V.

Within each part and the corresponding appendices you will find suggestions and support.

The various curricular demands on teachers can make it difficult to introduce drama as regularly as suggested in the calendar presented above. However, providing students with some drama-based experiences prior to the three-month series of lessons outlined below (and described in this book) is helpful preparation (but not necessary!).

This three-month calendar provides a series of weekly suggestions for implementing the activities from this book. More detailed schedules are provided in Part IV to offer specific production and rehearsal suggestions for teachers when bringing *Dream* to the stage.

Three-month Sample Calendar of Lessons and Strategies

MONTH 1

Monday	Tuesday	Wednesday	Thursday	Friday
	Role drama 1	Role drama 1	Role drama 2	Role drama 2
	Role drama 3	Role drama 3		
	Story session 1	Story session 2	Story session 3	
	Story session 4	Story session 5	Story session 6	

MONTH 2

Monday	Tuesday	Wednesday	Thursday	Friday
	Story session 7	Story session 8	Review of story	
	Read script	Read script	Read script	
	Rehearsal	Rehearsal	Rehearsal	
	Rehearsal	Rehearsal	Rehearsal	

MONTH 3

Monday	Tuesday	Wednesday	Thursday	Friday
	Rehearsal	Rehearsal	Rehearsal	
Rehearsal	Rehearsal	Rehearsal	Rehearsal	Rehearsal
Dress rehearsal	Dress rehearsal	Production	Production	

ADDITIONAL RESOURCES AND REFERENCES

Parts II, III, and IV provide a variety of detailed activities, and this is supported by Appendix A, where further activities and games are suggested. In addition, you might find the specific resources below helpful. A complete list of these and all other resources can be found at the back of the book.

Drama Strategies

A number of practical resources outlining drama strategies similar to those used in this book are available for teachers:

- Ackroyd and Boulton 2001
- Baldwin 2008, 2012
- Booth 2005
- Bowell and Heap 2001
- Hulson 2006
- Neelands 2004
- Miller and Saxton 2004
- O'Neill 1995
- Sinclair, Jeanneret, and O'Toole 2012
- Swartz and Nyman 2010

Drama Activities and Games for the Classroom

The following references are some useful sources for activities and games:

- Boal 2002
- Booth 1986
- Levy 2005
- Neelands and Goode 2000
- Novelly 1985
- Polsky 1989
- Pura 2002
- Scher and Verrall 1987
- Smith 2012
- Struthers 2005
- Swartz 2002
- Theodorou 1989

Drama Strategies and Shakespeare

The following references are teacher resources that focus on drama strategies specifically in relation to the study of Shakespearean plays:

- Ackroyd, Neelands, Supple, and Trowsdale 1998a; 1998b
- Belliveau and Prendergast 2013
- Clark, Dobson, Goode, and Neelands 1997

- » O'Neill and Lambert 1982
- » Weltsek 2005

Bringing Shakespeare to the Classroom

Other resources that complement this book are available to elementary teachers wishing to bring Shakespeare into their classrooms.

- » Joe Winston and Miles Tandy's (2012) *Beginning Shakespeare 4–11* provides readers with a thoughtful guide to introducing Shakespeare to young learners. Based on their work at the Royal Shakespeare Company and in schools in the United Kingdom, the authors provide practical and research knowledge for teachers, offering a number of entry points to begin working with a variety of Shakespearean plays.
- » John Doona's *A Practical Guide to Shakespeare for the Primary School* (2012) is equally useful for teachers, introducing specific strategies for young learners to engage with the work of Shakespeare in playful and meaningful ways.
- » Lois Burdett's Shakespeare Can Be Fun! series—including *A Midsummer Night's Dream for Kids* (1997)—presents primary teachers with lively, illustrated story versions of Shakespeare's plays written in rhyming couplets.
- » Richard Carter has adapted eight Shakespeare plays based on his years of working with young learners on Lopez Island, WA. His adaptations, such as for *A Midsummer Night's Dream* (2008), typically run 60–80 minutes and have been used around the world.
- » Online lesson plans and resources for working with Shakespeare in elementary classrooms are available through the:
  - Folger Institute in Washington, DC (www.folger.edu)
  - Royal Shakespeare Company, UK (www.rsc.org.uk)

Readers' Theatre

To build oral language fluency in the play-preparation period, you might include Readers' Theatre. Many students enjoy reading age-appropriate Readers' Theatre scripts in small groups, and doing so helps them understand some of the conventions of theatre scripts. You might consult the following references:

- » Campbell and Cleland 2003
- » Poulsen 2012
- » Wolfman 2004
- » Young and Rasinski 2009

PART II

DISCOVERING SHAKESPEARE AND *A MIDSUMMER NIGHT'S DREAM*

STUDENTS DO NOT NEED TO HAVE ANY EXPERIENCE WITH THE PLAY *Dream* or with Shakespeare to engage in the three role dramas found in Part II. The role dramas are intended to ease students into their exploration of the author and the world of the play. As well, they help to develop confidence with drama.

As students will learn, William Shakespeare was born some time before April 26, 1564 and baptised on that date in Stratford-upon-Avon in England. He died in April 1616. Shakespeare was a poet, playwright, and actor, working in London and most famously at the Globe Theatre. He wrote comedies, tragedies, and history plays, and is known for his inventive use of language; in fact, in Shakespeare's works, hundreds of words appear in written English for the first time ever.

As a romantic comedy, the play *A Midsummer Night's Dream* has people of three worlds collide:

1. the royal court of ancient Athens, including Theseus the Duke and the woman he will soon marry, Hippolyta, as well as four young Athenians who are romantically entangled (Hermia, Helena, Lysander, and Demetrius) and Hermia's father, Egeus
2. a group of workers who wish to present a play to Theseus and Hippolyta for their wedding celebration—including Quince, Snug, Bottom, Flute, Snout, and Starveling
3. the fairy world existing in the wood near Athens—including Oberon (the king), Titania (the queen), Puck (who serves Oberon), and other fairies

ROLE DRAMAS

Role dramas generally consist of a sequence of drama-based activities that build one upon the other to generate belief in and commitment to a given topic. The group-oriented activities suggested below are easy to use for those less familiar with drama-based approaches to learning. Prior to beginning the role dramas, you

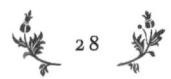

might engage your class with one or two warm-up activities, such as the games in Appendix A.

Each role drama is divided into scenes to mark a shift in dramatic activity. In each scene, a new tactic is used to build tension; to gather, analyze, and disseminate information; to facilitate problem solving; or to resolve the conflict or crisis. The activity within a scene can be individually focused, but the majority of scenes are designed so that students are engaged in group work. The scenes culminate in an outcome that is not predetermined but rather decided by the whole group working together as the role drama unfolds.

Note that the term "scene" has the additional meaning of a scene in a play. In role drama, a group may be asked to prepare an unscripted scene for presentation. Such scenes might be referred to by students and teachers as "skits," but this term fails to reflect the serious effort and thoughtful reflection required.

Students in Role

Many students are familiar with "improv games," in which the activity is designed to show cleverness, humour, or teamwork, or follow a specified formula. Other drama activities might focus on developing students as actors. In contrast, the goals of improvising or being in role are to explore and investigate, observe what is happening, and respond in ways that are congruent with the role assigned. Improvisation or role play is unscripted and allows students to "think on their feet," as well as to interact in role during group work when problem solving or planning an activity. For students who spend all day *being* students, improvisation in role offers an opportunity to explore the roles and responsibilities of individuals in a variety of situations and contexts. In the three role dramas that follow, students are asked to enter into role at various points within the activities.

Teachers in Role

What tasks does a teacher undertake in role drama? A teacher in role challenges, questions, shapes, and focuses the inquiry from within the role drama by adopting a particular role and point of view. A teacher in role may take on a role of a leader, facilitator, guide, advisor, stranger, or bystander. However, rather than being an authoritative figure dictating the action, whenever possible the teacher in role should guide others (students) to become decision makers or advisors. The teacher in role sets the situation and context, proposes new dilemmas when and if necessary, and helps students interact in role by remaining in role as well. The challenge of being in role is to avoid directing the role drama in the way that you want or anticipate that it should go. Students should feel that they are the ones who are making decisions in role.

USING THE ROLE DRAMAS

In the role dramas that follow, the teacher script is shown in *italics*, with additional instructions indicated in normal (non-italic) text. Terms that are included in the glossary are shown in **boldface**.

- Each of the three role dramas below is self-contained and stands on its own.
- The role dramas last anywhere between 60 and 90 minutes each, depending on how much time a class wishes to spend on each activity.
- Possible extensions and variations to role dramas often emerge from something a particular group has done or questions students ask that deserve further investigation. As you gain more experience and confidence leading role dramas, you can alter the activities to suit the needs and leads of your class.
- If possible, an open space with room to move around is preferred for all the role dramas.
- A variety of individual drama strategies are introduced in this part. Appendix A provides more elaborate descriptions for some activities.
- Low-risk activities, those where students can easily engage, feel confident, be less vulnerable emotionally, physically, and/or vocally, are deliberately used at the beginning of the role dramas to ease students into the work.
- Some of the activities have sections in italics to indicate the teacher's talk. These represent suggested teacher scripts to provide instructions during the role dramas, and they may be adapted and expanded as needed.
- For each of the three role dramas, you will find the following:
  - an entry point
  - a description of the imagined situation that underpins the role drama
  - a list of roles and tasks
  - a list of needed materials
  - an overview of the role drama with strategies noted
  - the role drama, with scene-by-scene support
  - suggestions for debriefing and reflections
  - curricular objectives
  - extensions and variations
  - assessment
  - comments from teachers and researchers about the role drama in action

The following references are some useful additional sources that introduce role drama, process drama, or story drama:

- » Booth 2005
- » Bowell and Heap 2001
- » Fels and Belliveau 2008
- » Miller and Saxton 2004
- » O'Neill 1995
- » Tarlington and Verriour 1991

ROLE DRAMA 1: WHO ART THOU SHAKESPEARE?

This role drama gives students the opportunity to discover a little about Shakespeare's life, plays, and legacy, and the Globe Theatre. The role drama helps students realize that what is known about Shakespeare is often contested. The activities aim to generate a sense of ensemble and teamwork as well as curiosity about Shakespeare. The role drama makes playful use of the clichéd excuse or joke that "my dog ate my homework."

Author's Perspective: Entry Point—Controversy about Shakespeare

A few years ago, I read a book-length account of William-Henry Ireland's forgeries of Shakespeare (Pierce 2004) and his role as one of many meddlers in Shakespeare's legacy. In 1795, Mr. Ireland introduced what he claimed was an undiscovered Shakespearean play, *Vortigern*. With the help of some influential London citizens, a full stage production of the play opened at the Drury Lane Theatre. Critics of the day quickly realized the play was not by Shakespeare, but a forgery, and the production closed after just one performance. Over 200 years later, controversy about Shakespeare's work continues in both academic and popular work. One example is the film *Anonymous*, directed by Roland Emmerich (2011), which depicts the Earl of Oxford as the writer of plays credited to Shakespeare. The ongoing debate over whether or not Shakespeare wrote the plays credited to him suggests that there is always some mystery around Shakespeare and some room for interpretation. For over 400 years, historians, other scholars, and artists (and forgers) have been piecing together facts and theories about Shakespeare and his work.

This role drama focusing on an imagined conference about Shakespeare encourages students to work collaboratively, piecing together bits of information about Shakespeare so that they can share *their* knowledge. Participating in role in conference presentations offers students an ideal opportunity and motivation to practise their listening and communication skills.

The Imagined Situation

Renowned Elizabethan scholar Dr. Pierce Shaker, a professor at the University of Wittenberg, is in town to give a talk to teachers about his new book about Shakespeare. You (the teacher) are his niece or nephew. Dr. Shaker settled into a local hotel and left his loyal dog Iago to sleep peacefully on the bed while he went for dinner. He also leaves behind his handwritten manuscript—handwritten because he feared computers. Upon his return to the room, Dr. Shaker finds that his manuscript for *The Story of Shakespeare* is torn to shreds. Iago is lying on one of the pillows, slyly grinning, with pieces of paper sticking out of his mouth. Dr. Shaker speculates that, as soon as he left for dinner, Iago used his social network to have a party in the hotel room with fellow canines: Little Rich, Lady Beth, T-Bolt, and others. Deeply distressed at seeing 10 years of work torn to pieces by his faithful companion, Dr. Shaker asks you (the teacher) to work with your students to piece together parts of the book for tomorrow's talk. Additionally, students are to present a speech from *Dream* at the conference.

> **ROLES AND TASKS**
> » teacher in role as Dr. Shaker's niece or nephew
> » students in role as dogs, objects, Dr. Shaker, researchers, reporters, and presenters
>
> **MATERIALS**
> » artifacts about Shakespeare (e.g., books, posters for plays, pictures of the Globe Theatre) collected from your school or local library or the Internet, and printed
> » copy of the poster for the conference with details added (see Appendix B)
> » copies of Puck's speech, "If we shadows have offended" (see Appendix B)
> » copies of the postcard for the conference (see Appendix B)
> » stickers to colour-code: red, blue, green, black, purple, yellow
> » facts about Shakespeare on loose paper, cut into narrow strips: one fact per strip, colour-coded (see Appendix B)
> » six large sheets of paper posted on the wall with titles
> » markers

Overview: Scenes and Drama Strategies

SCENE 1 Rehearsing Puck's speech, "If we shadows have offended" (**choric voices**)
SCENE 2 Dr. Shaker's tragic moment (**mime**, re-enactment, storytelling)
SCENE 3 Fact-finding (role-playing)
SCENE 4 Reporters and researchers (**interviewing**)
SCENE 5 Preparing the presentation (**tableaux, play-building, dress rehearsal, choric voices**)
SCENE 6 Conference (presenting in role)

The Role Drama
SCENE 1: *Rehearsing Puck's speech, "If we shadows have offended"*
Prepare the classroom so that, as students enter the classroom, they see artifacts about Shakespeare and copies of the poster for the upcoming Shakespeare conference. (Alternatively, display the poster with a projector or create a poster on the board.) Inform students that they have been invited to do a small performance for this conference. The class is to perform Puck's final speech from *Dream*, "If we shadows have offended." Provide copies of the speech to students or project the speech on a screen.

Have the class read the text out loud as a group a few times. Then, working collectively with your students, brainstorm ways of using their voices and bodies to creatively bring the text to life. During this time, drop a few hints that this is an important conference and that the main speaker, Dr. Shaker, happens to be your dear uncle. His work on Shakespeare is very important and well known, and tomorrow he will share some material from his forthcoming book, *The Story of Shakespeare*. Point to the poster, which highlights this information for students.

SCENE 2: *News about Uncle*
Imagine that you receive the following message from your uncle: "Dearest niece/nephew, please call my hotel room. Something horrible has happened." When you call your uncle, he describes how he went for dinner and returned to his room to find that the pages of his book were torn and scattered on the floor.

In preparation, place the loose, colour-coded strips of paper with facts about Shakespeare in the classroom.

Tell your students that you will describe in detail what your uncle thinks happened. Ask them to participate in a mimed, slow-motion re-enactment of what might have taken place in Dr. Shaker's hotel room. Have students sit in a large circle and use the centre as the area where the story will be recreated. Use the script that follows to engage in a "physicalized" storytelling activity. As you retell your uncle's story, invite your students with gentle prompting in and out of the scene so that they enter the playing area to depict objects (e.g., radio, telephone, TV) and characters (Iago and his dog friends) that you mention. You might prompt them by asking what music or program was on the radio: *Could someone help create this music or talk show?* You might also prepare one or two students before the role drama with specific ideas and a tentative script. An example of a prepared script for a student could include: *As a **nightlight**, I remembered being quietly turned off. Then all was calm. All of a sudden, I was turned on, as were all the rest of my light friends in the room. Loud music was playing, the TV was blasting, phones were ringing, and animals were coming in and out of the room. I was shaking and* *blinking from all the noise and movement. Then after an hour or two, all went dark and quiet again.*

This storytelling activity, which students animate with mime, will help them to imagine and create the hotel room. When you reach a point where the scene needs to be cleared, ask students in the playing area to return to the outer circle. You can begin again with a new set of students depicting and building on what might have happened in the hotel room from the perspective of the objects and animals. The key events that might have happened are as follows, but revise if needed to suit your classroom context and needs.

NOTE: Extended teacher script is in italics with other instructions in normal (non-italic) text.

The hotel room has a large bed, desk, chair, TV, radio, telephone, and the unpublished book. Invite students to become part of this setting.

Dr. Shaker leaves the hotel room while Iago, his dog, is pretending to sleep on the bed.

As the door shuts, Iago turns on the lights, TV, and radio and picks up the phone to quickly contact his network of dog friends.

By this time it is important to have one student playing Iago.

His friends arrive, and the TV and music are loud. The dogs play and dance wildly and the scene escalates into a dog party that is out of control. Somehow the precious book manuscript is ripped and its pages scattered all over the floor. This should be done in mime and slow motion using the loose colour-coded strips of paper already placed in the classroom. Try to have students scatter the strips of paper randomly around the room.

As Dr. Shaker is heard fiddling with the key in the door, all goes quiet and the dog friends hide underneath the bed. Iago returns to his original position on the bed, yawning, but with a piece of paper still in his mouth.

Dr. Shaker looks around and everything is scattered on the floor, including his book in pieces. He screams in horror. Encourage the student in role as Dr. Shaker to freeze in a tableau, like that seen in Edvard Munch's *The Scream*.

SCENE 3: *Fact-finding: Trying to Piece Together the Puzzle*
In advance, prepare the postcards about the conference so that each student will receive one and each card will be colour-coded with a sticker to create equal-sized groups: red, blue, green, black, purple, yellow. Use these colours to divide students into groups.

» **RED GROUP**   Shakespeare's early life and family

- » **BLUE GROUP**   Shakespeare's language, plots, and plays
- » **GREEN GROUP**   Shakespeare's comedies
- » **BLACK GROUP**   Shakespeare's tragedies
- » **PURPLE GROUP** Shakespeare's Globe Theatre
- » **YELLOW GROUP** Shakespeare's influence

Ask each group to look in the classroom for the pages with facts about Shakespeare (used in Scene 2) and that match their group colour. For example, the group with postcards with red stickers will look for the red-coded pages, so gather information about Shakespeare's early life and family.

Tell the students that Dr. Shaker's hotel room is a crime scene—where Iago and friends destroyed Dr. Shaker's work—so they must not remove the papers. Ask them instead to individually record at least three facts for their group on the back of a postcard. Members from each colour group will undoubtedly record some of the same facts as other members of their group.

SCENE 4: *Reporters and Researchers*

Tape six large, colour-coded pieces of paper onto the wall with the following six titles:

- » Early life and family
- » Language, plots, and plays
- » Comedies
- » Tragedies
- » Globe Theatre
- » Influence

Assign half the class to role play reporters and the other half to role play researchers who share their findings with the reporters. They will later switch roles. (If you wish, you could divide the class using colour groups—e.g., red, blue, and green group students play reporters first and then researchers, while black, purple, and yellow do the reverse. However, note that *every* student will play both a reporter and a researcher.) Invite researchers to sit in different places around the imagined hotel room with their postcards and found facts; ask reporters to move about to interview at least four or five researchers. Instruct students to switch roles so that the new reporters also interview four or five researchers.

When this activity is completed, invite everyone to sit in a circle. Ask each student to state at least one fact that he or she discovered during the interviews.

Then ask students to write down as much information as they can remember from their reporter roles onto the chart papers hung on the walls. *Now, in role as reporters, please list on the sheets of paper facts about the six topics.* Instruct students to start by writing three pieces of information and then to try to add more without repeating a fact that appears on a sheet already. Remind students not to correct one another as they write on the sheets. This is second-hand information, and as such, might be interpreted and possibly misinterpreted during interviews. Students should not, however, exaggerate or purposefully write down incorrect information that they heard.

SCENE 5: *Preparing for the Conference*

In role as Dr. Shaker's niece or nephew, explain to your class that, because of your uncle's misfortunes, he is too distressed to present his talk on Shakespeare. However, you told the organizer that you have a perfect solution to this problem. *With the help of my students, I think we might be able to share some things about Shakespeare at the conference, such as his early life, his plays, his legacy, and other things. I'll ask my students how they might help.*

Guide students to return to their colour-coded groups to prepare for the conference. Instruct students to look at the sheet of paper for their group's focus to see what their peers understood from the researcher/reporter role play. This allows students to compare what they know from their fact-finding and see possible misinterpretations. The focus on one theme or topic about Shakespeare and presenting each through drama is also a form of play-building.

Tell students that their job is now to find creative ways to share three pieces of information about their topic. For instance, the blue group (language, plots, and plays) might share how Shakespeare: 1) uses poetry; 2) was inventive in his language; and 3) used older, known stories for some plots.

To help students vocally share their findings, ask each group to create at least three tableaux, one for each piece of information. Remind students that a tableau can involve sound and movement, so theirs are talking tableaux. If students are not accustomed to doing tableau work, you might have to provide suggestions and/or examples. Allow students five to seven minutes to work on the selection of facts and creation of tableaux. Then, hold a full-class dress rehearsal for groups to practise simultaneously how each group wishes to share its three talking tableaux. The purpose of this is not to present to the other groups but to work out any difficulties in the presentation. The dress rehearsal should take about 45 seconds, during which each group practises each of its three tableaux. Depending on your students' experience with tableaux, you may need to provide hands-on guidance and/or ask them to undertake a few dress rehearsals.

After the dress rehearsal, return to the "If we shadows..." speech and rehearse the piece using choric voices and simple group body movements. For example, have students form two wide lines, one behind the other (as in a class photo). The front group could speak the first two lines of the speech as they slowly take four steps forwards. The back group could speak the next two lines as they take four steps forwards. The next two lines can be done while the front group kneels, and so on. The idea is to keep the movement and voice work simple and group-oriented. Inform students that this speech will be the final piece of their presentation at the conference. The order for the conference presentation should be similar to the list in Scene 3 (i.e., red group—Shakespeare's early life and family—goes first, followed by blue group—Shakespeare's language, plots, and plays, and so on), with the addition of the "If we shadows…" speech at the very end.

SCENE 6: *Conference and Discussion*
In role as Dr. Shaker's niece or nephew, explain to an imaginary conference audience that you and your class will be sharing a presentation about Shakespeare, replacing your uncle who suffered a minor setback. Before beginning the presentations, make sure everyone is ready. Ensuring this may entail another dress rehearsal. Orchestrate the six colour-coded groups to share their talking tableaux with facts about Shakespeare. This leads into the entire class presenting the "If we shadows…" speech.

After the tableaux and speech, have students sit in a large circle to discuss any questions or comments that arose from the presentation. The students may have questions or require clarifications about the facts collected from each group.

Debriefing and Reflections

The Scene 6 discussion leads naturally to a **debriefing** in which students share their thoughts and feelings about their experience in the role drama.

» *What issues, ideas, thoughts, opinions, or insights came up for you during the role drama?*
» *Are there any questions that remained unanswered?*

Students might talk about facts they discovered, how people interpret things in different ways, or the experience of working as a group. They might talk about Dr. Shaker and the goal of conferences. If time permits, you might wish to ask students to write or draw a reflection about their individual experiences. For example:

» *What are three things you learned today aside from those you wrote on your postcard?*

> » *What are three things you remember/enjoyed doing today?*
> » *What ideas that you had previously about Shakespeare changed as a result of doing this activity?*
> » *What experiences have you had with drama so far in your life?*

You may also steer students towards more critical thinking responses.

> » *Do you think it was right of us as a class to interpret Dr. Shaker's work?*
> » *Should we have checked with him before presenting at the conference? Why?*

Curricular Objectives

This role drama cuts across various curricular areas, including language arts, social studies, and drama. For example, students can locate England and Stratford-upon-Avon on a map. As a class, students could consider what was happening in the late 16th and early 17th centuries, reflecting on what they know about that time period. They might also talk about the language of Shakespeare or references they have heard about the playwright.

At the heart of these activities is the desire to encourage students' curiosity and pleasure in learning. Unlike many secondary school students, early learners typically do not have preconceived negative impressions about Shakespeare. As such, a positive, empowering early experience with Shakespeare is an important step to help lessen the fear of Shakespeare in later years. In this role drama, students have the chance to role play in groups and individually, exploring an "as if" world, and so to exercise their imagination and creativity. They are also asked to gather and choose among key facts about Shakespeare, and then in groups decide which ones they would like to share. These activities build communication, interviewing, and decision-making skills, as well as group work skills. The role drama introduces students to various drama strategies, including mime, choric voice, story enactment, tableaux, and performance. These strategies support key curricular objectives involving speaking, listening, reading, and responding. The debriefing at the end also allows time for students to orally express their thoughts and feelings, followed by opportunities to write or draw these in a reflective journal.

Extensions and Variations

This role drama is specifically designed to introduce Shakespeare, yet the activities could be used to introduce another writer, or a composer, artist, or significant event. For instance, your class could explore Claude Monet and piece together aspects of his life and art using reproductions of one or more paintings. Or, you could explore Pythagoras' life, the Pythagoreans, and the discovery of π (pi).

As a variation, you might decide to add to or change the focus of the facts about Shakespeare—for example, by including facts about the history plays.

Extensions within this role drama are also possible in a few select places. For example, adding a **hot seating** activity could help the class dig deeper. The class could hot seat Iago (the dog) to ask what happened in the hotel room from his perspective. Were Dr. Shaker and Iago loyal friends? Did something recently happen in their relationship? There could also be a section in the role drama where students brainstorm different sessions for the conference, imagining what could be presented. If the class wanted to further explore the concept of interpretations and misinterpretations, you could ask them to use the large sheets of paper from Scene 4 where second-hand information was slightly altered from the original information. A role play about a new "interpretation" about Shakespeare's life and works could be explored.

Assessment

There are a variety of formal and informal ways of assessing student learning and engagement in drama. However, it is important to recognize that learning through/in drama is not always visible. A number of students will take on a role in a very private manner, committing to it without outwardly showing their investment. Conversely, some of the more extroverted students might give the impression of being committed, without truly being engaged in the role drama activities. Knowing your students is key. Some questions for informal assessment can include:

» Did this student participate collaboratively during the planning lessons of the group?
» Was the student supportive of others' suggestions?
» Did the student offer insightful ideas?
» Did the work incorporate the concepts, ideas, information, or perceptions that are being explored?

If students wrote reflections in role following a role drama or presentation, these can be assessed using more formal modes. These written (or illustrated) comments may be evaluated in terms of the ability of a student to show evidence of understanding, thoughtful insight, and application of content knowledge through critical thinking and creative play. Peer evaluation and self-evaluation provide another way for you to evaluate student learning and work, along with ongoing observation.

This role drama on Shakespeare is intended to build ensemble and group playing skills. As such, the assessment should include informal observations on how individuals help foster positive group dynamics.

> » How did students contribute to their group?
> » What ideas did they contribute?
> » What ideas from their peers were they able to support?

The assessment should be about helping students be more successful with group work and encourage a collaborative, ensemble atmosphere in the classroom.

> I have used a variety of ways to introduce Shakespeare to my students, and I never really felt successful as I was merely listing a bunch of facts. I once invited a parent with a rich literature background in Shakespeare and that worked quite well, as she brought images and hidden facts. This role drama, though, gave ownership to the students to discover Shakespeare. They became the experts about his life and plays. Through the role-playing, they were invested and committed to learning and sharing their "facts." The activities were playful, and as one of the students said in the debriefing, "It was really kind of weird to think we were learning about history, but yet we were play-acting!" Learning through drama engaged them and was a great way to get to know a little about Shakespeare before we started working on the play. It was a way for me to have them "buy in" to Shakespeare. —TEACHER

> In observing this role drama on a few occasions, what I found most striking was the ownership in the decision making students took regarding their learning. This supports Heathcote's "mantle of the expert" (Heathcote and Bolton 1995) approach where students take on important roles as information seekers and conveyors of knowledge. The activity also pushes students towards meaningful transmediation (Siegel 1995) as they translate their interpretation of words into mimed movement and tableaux. The mystery and unresolved nature of the work maintains student interest and generates intrigue as students create their own scenes about what they know (O'Neill 1995).
> —RESEARCHER/OBSERVER

ROLE DRAMA 2: ATHENIAN MARKET

The heart of this role drama is ensemble and group work, combined with students beginning to learn about how to put a play together in a class. As well, this role drama invites students inside the world of *Dream* by introducing the language of Shakespeare along with some scenes and characters from the play. Students require no previous experience with *Dream*. Parts of this role drama extend beyond the events within *Dream*. You might note that the play combines aspects of two eras:

it was written around 1600 in England, was set in ancient Greece, and combines certain occupations found in England under Queen Elizabeth I (who reigned 1558–1603).

Author's Perspective: Entry Point—Non-actors Performing

While doing my master's degree at the University of Toronto, I took a course in drama education with Dr. David Booth. This is where I was awakened to the numerous possibilities of introducing drama and theatre to a *wide* audience of learners. Until then I had studied solely in theatre departments where the objective was to generate and produce professional theatre. The art form was reserved for the trained artist. My introduction to drama education with Dr. Booth sparked my desire to understand how concepts of theatre and drama can (and should!) be introduced into any classroom. I quickly realized that my work in drama education involved modifying and repurposing my theatre training, and adjusting and scaffolding the activities, but by no means diminishing the art form or my training. Introducing non-theatre teachers and students to drama activities continues to be a core commitment within my teaching and research. Enabling teachers and students to explore new ways of learning and to rekindle the joy of play is at the centre of this role drama.

The Situation

A grand wedding for the Duke and Duchess is about to take place in Athens, and a call has been made for a competition between local towns to perform a play at the celebration. (This playful competition is not part of Shakespeare's actual play, but an extension of *Dream*.) The local people have many different jobs from Shakespeare's era, and the job list you will share with students will be an introduction to the many different occupations during Shakespeare's life. (If you wish, you or the students could research more jobs.) In role as Peter Quince, you will guide your class, which will be in role as a group of amateur actors hoping to perform at the Duke's palace.

> **ROLES AND TASKS**
> » teacher in role as Peter Quince
> » students in role as local people, actors
>
> **MATERIALS**
> » colour copies of the leaf template, one per student, and using four to six colours equally (see Appendix C)
> » images and books that feature Athens, Greece
> » music of Greece, sound effects of a marketplace, sounds of a trumpet or horns to announce your arrival (optional)

> » job list (see Appendix C) either projected for students or displayed in some other way in the classroom
> » markers and masking tape or safety pins
> » copies of Scenes for Athenian Market Role Drama and Instructions, copied so each student will have a copy of the scene for his or her group (see Appendix C)

Overview: Scenes and Drama Strategies
SCENE 1 Welcome to nearby Athens (**visualization**)
SCENE 2 Names and occupations (role play)
SCENE 3 A play to be performed (teacher in role, **tableaux**)
SCENE 4 What led to this? (**flashback, dress rehearsal**)
SCENE 5 Putting the pieces together (**play-building**)

The Role Drama

SCENE 1: *Welcome to Nearby Athens*

Prepare by displaying different coloured leaves around the classroom, one for each student, and by displaying images of, and books about, Athens and Greece. (If it is available, you might also play Greek music.) Display a list of jobs found in 16th- and 17th-century England for students to see as they enter the classroom.

Ask students to lie on the floor in a comfortable place and lead them in a visualization activity. Ask them to listen to the following excerpt from a script and visualize the scene you describe. Adapt the visualization as needed:

Our story takes place a time long ago in a small town near Athens, Greece, near the seaside. You are part of a bustling community, with many people coming and going, trading their goods in the marketplace. The town has many shops and many people with all sorts of occupations: bakeries with bakers making bread and pastries, cobblers who fix shoes, and carpenters who build homes. This is a humble town—meaning you're not wealthy but you have enough—and you lead a satisfying life. Imagine that you are a worker in this town. You have your little shop and regular customers come in. Pause

Over on the top of the hill is the Duke's palace, a place you have never been because, as townspeople, you're never invited to the palace. You've always wanted to go there—everyone would like to go! You have heard that it's the most beautiful place in all of Greece. The palace overlooks all the towns and villages, the big city of Athens, and the sea. The people at the palace wear beautiful clothes. The palace has plenty of fresh food and shade from the heat, and there is always a festive atmosphere. One day you hope to go! Pause

In the meantime, you keep doing your job—such as mending clothes or selling vegetables.

You could revise this script to include more occupations that will be familiar to students and some that will be new and intriguing.

Gradually lead students to quietly stand up and walk in the space in the centre of the room.

SCENE 2: *Names and Occupations*
The classroom is now a marketplace where all the workers of the town come to meet, exchange their goods, catch up on gossip, and hear the latest news. If you wish, play music or the sound effects of a bustling marketplace. Using the displayed job list from Shakespeare's time, guide your students to choose a job to role play.

You might choose one of the listed jobs, or make up your own. Once you have a job, create a fictional name for yourself. You might be Camilo the carpenter or Wendy the weaver, for example.

Ask students to greet one another in the imagined marketplace by shaking hands or saying "hello," and introducing themselves by name and occupation as they walk through the space. In doing so, they gradually assume a role.

Try to meet at least four or five other workers from your town. You may want to try a new name for yourself, changing it as you move about, to find the one that suits you.

Ask students to explore different walks, that is, to experiment walking in different ways. *Walk very slowly, on your toes, bent over, skipping.*

Explore these walks and others for a minute or so with students. *Now try to discover and decide how your character walks.*

Guide students to continue walking in the space to explore how their characters might walk. *Do you walk hunched over? Do you take small steps? Do you walk tall?*

After a few moments, ask everyone to stop.

Instruct students to randomly choose one of the colour-coded leaves that you set out earlier and then to write their chosen job title and character name on the leaf. (The colour-coding of the leaves helps students form the groups for the next scene.) Next, ask students to tape (or safety-pin) the leaves to their shirts.

SCENE 3: *A Play To Be Performed*
In role as Peter Quince, enter the classroom triumphantly and full of excitement. (You may choose to use the sounds of trumpets or horns to announce your entrance.)

The Duke is getting married to the beautiful Hippolyta! It is to be the wedding of the century. To help celebrate, the Duke is going to have a lavish event at the palace. A part of this celebration will be a theatre performance, and—this is the exciting news—he is inviting each town in the region to propose a play. The winning town will perform their play for the wedding and be given the royal treatment at the palace. I think our town can be the one chosen, but we will need everyone's full help and support.

Ask the students, who are now in role as townspeople, to help out. This will help build belief and your enthusiasm will win them over.

So, here's my plan. I have a few brief scenes from a play I once saw in Athens. I managed to copy parts of it. We'll divide into groups and rehearse these.

Use the colour-coded leaves with the students' character names to divide them into groups. Adapt the instructions with names and colours—first blue, then green, and so on. As you form each group, give the group its scene:

Now Alexandro, you and the rest of the blue leaves will look at this scene....

Cleopatra, you and the rest of the green leaves will have this scene...

Continue in this fashion until all students/groups have their own scenes.

There should be four to six groups divided by colours, each with a brief scene to present along with instructions. If students are unfamiliar with tableaux, you may wish to prepare a group prior to class to demonstrate an example.

Now that you have your groups, I want you to rehearse these short scenes. Now, I heard that the other towns are only using their voices—to read the words in the scene aloud—but I think that if we also physically portray the scenes, we might be chosen to perform our play! In each scene, you might have one or more readers, but let's add at least one tableau to show the story as well.

In role as Quince, assist each group in rehearsing their tableau. After a few minutes of rehearsing, ask that two groups come together to share their scenes with one another and provide feedback. For example, the blue leaves group would present their piece to the yellow leaves, the yellow group members give feedback, then the yellow group presents to the blue, and the blue group gives feedback.

SCENE 4: *What Led to This?*

In role as Peter Quince again, set out another task for the student groups: to create a tableau that shows what happened before their first tableau.

While you were rehearsing, I snuck into the next town (disguised, of course) to observe the competition and they were doing the same thing—small scenes and tableaux. We need to stand out if we are going to win the competition and be selected for the wedding. While walking back I had a thought, a clever idea! Let's try to imagine what happened before your scene. I would like you to create a second tableau. In this tableau, show what might have happened before your scene—like a prequel or flashback. Once you have created the flashback, find a way to make a transition from your new tableau to your previous tableau to show the story. No words are necessary for the flashback tableau.

STEPPING INTO DRAMA

In role as Quince, go from group to group to support and offer feedback on the flashback ideas. Encourage students to be creative. After a few moments, invite two groups to share with the rest of the class what they have done so far, that is, each group's flashback tableau and scene tableau. This can develop into a practice and dress rehearsal opportunity.

SCENE 5: *Putting the Pieces Together*

It is now time to put the group pieces together. In advance, determine the order in which your students will share their scenes—preferably chronologically as they appear within Shakespeare's play (and in Appendix C), as this will help with flow from one group to the next. Instruct students to share comments about their two flashback tableaux.

If time permits, you may ask students to comment on what they see in the tableaux. Make clear to the student audiences that their goal is to form their own interpretations or impressions rather than trying to guess or figure out what people are doing, such as in a game of charades. You can also ask the creators of the tableaux to make a brief comment about their work and interpretation. This might be a time to remind students that tableaux need not be literal or obvious: the focus of the activity is a representation, an impression.

As the last group completes their tableaux, in role as Quince, let them know the following news:

I just received some fantastic news! The Duke's men were secretly watching as we rehearsed our play, and it is preferred! Our play was chosen! We will be going to perform for the Duke and Duchess on their wedding night! In the palace!

Debriefing and Reflections

Begin the debriefing by staying in role as Quince and townspeople to wonder what it will be like to perform for the Duke and Duchess.

» *What will the palace look like?*
» *Should we make costumes for our play?*
» *What made the Duke's men prefer our play over the others?*
» *What did we do that made them choose us?*

Moving out of role, begin **debriefing** the class about the role drama.

» *What was your experience as a participant or player in your scene?*
» *Do you have questions about the content or characters?*
» *In looking back, how did you decide on your flashback ideas?*

> What connections did you see between each group's scenes?
> What connections did you see between this drama and our last role drama about Shakespeare?

You might ask students to write about their imagined experience of performing at the Duke's palace. They can write and/or draw about how the play unfolded for the Duke and Duchess at the wedding, how it was received, and what they experienced at the wedding celebration and in the palace. This writing may take the form of an imagined journal entry or a letter to a fellow townsperson who did not get the opportunity to visit the palace.

Curricular Objectives

This role drama is designed to provide students with a glimpse at some of the characters, scenes, and language from *Dream*. It is intended to create an opportunity for students to immerse themselves in the world of the play, in particular exposing the class to the jobs of those who prepare and perform the play within the play *Dream*. The activity allows students to discover some of the occupations during Shakespeare's era as well as the societal distinction between the commoners and the court.

The key literacy strands are emphasized as students read, write, speak, listen, and communicate in various ways in the activities. They are asked to communicate their understanding through both voice and body as they engage with tableau work. They are also asked to make inferences through the flashback activity. They look for clues as they predict and determine what might have happened beforehand. They build on their knowledge of how stories are constructed. As well, the focus on working in groups helps learners find ways to offer their input and to accept ideas from others.

Extensions and Variations

This role drama could be adapted to include more scenes from the play or use different ones, involve another work of fiction, or present a historical moment where a group of people are preparing for an event. Variations within the role drama could include selecting narrative excerpts from the abbreviated story instead of pieces from the play script. An alternative to the flashback could be a flash-forward/sequel, thus encouraging students to predict what the scenes might lead to.

Assessment

This role drama exposes students to some characters, scenes, and language of *Dream*. As such, the assessment should focus primarily on informal observations of how individuals are beginning to engage with the story. Written responses after the debriefing invite students to write in a creative manner. You might also discover how committed your students were to the activity.

For more about assessment of the role dramas, see Role Drama 1: Who Art Thou Shakespeare? (page 31).

> My students became very excited about the wedding! It was a great hook. They were genuinely enthused about the possibility of attending. I also had fun playing Peter Quince and getting them excited about doing the play. As I look back on that role drama, [I think] it really helped to shape aspects of our production of the play. We came to know some of the characters and the language but most importantly we worked as an ensemble in hopes of being chosen to play for the Duke's wedding. It also gave me the idea to play Peter Quince in the play, which was a perfect role in many ways. He is the one who motivates the workers to do the play, and he is very much of a supporter, cheerleader. —TEACHER

> This role drama helps students embrace roles as they become performers, directors, and playwrights/dramaturges [rescripting a past scene]. The teacher takes on these various roles as well through Peter Quince, along with pedagogically leading the activity. Bowell and Heap (2005) have conceptualized the idea of quadripartite thinking, which theorizes the multiple roles teachers and students engage in while doing role drama work (actor, playwright, director, leader). One role never truly takes precedence because, as soon as you've worked through one role, you're on to the next, but you still maintain the initial role(s). The layering, multi-tasking within role drama highlights and makes use of students' multiple ways of knowing and creative doing (Cramer, Ortlieb, and Cheek 2007; Gardner 2000). —RESEARCHER/OBSERVER

ROLE DRAMA 3: CHARACTER MASKS

This mask-making role drama invites students to explore the characters from *Dream*. The series of activities allows students to become more familiar with the characters and predict what the play is about. (A different version of this role drama is presented in Belliveau and Prendergast, 2013.)

Author's Perspective: Entry Point—All Those Characters!

I remember first being introduced to *Hamlet* in secondary school and being completely overwhelmed when looking at the character list, the dramatis personae. So many characters to remember! Who is Francisco? Horatio? Bernardo? Is there a

Ghost, really! I kept this in mind when I began teaching Shakespeare in schools. To try to avoid the feeling of being discouraged by the first page, I sought creative ways to help my students enter Shakespeare's plays. While teaching in middle school, I was also doing graduate work and one of my courses was on *commedia dell'arte*, a tradition that emerged in 16th century Italy. The course involved workshops on creating *commedia* character masks, and I saw the rich possibilities of integrating mask-making into a Shakespeare unit. Combining the Italian mask-making tradition with Shakespeare seemed a logical and artistic way to introduce my students to the extensive cast of characters. Familiarizing them with the names of the characters—and placing the characters in various "worlds" or clusters—helped ease my students into Shakespeare's plays.

The Situation

The artistic director of our Summer Shakespeare Festival has asked for a class of local children to help in an upcoming production of *Dream*. The class will present a prelude to a production in the Summer Festival to introduce specific moments within the play.

ROLES AND TASKS
- teacher as facilitator, role-playing *Dream* characters
- students in role as characters from *Dream*

MATERIALS
- character masks copied for each student, cut or not (see Appendix D)
- dramatis personae with brief descriptions for *Dream* (see Appendix D)
- slips of paper for character names in three different colours
- basket
- paper, markers, crayons, scissors, glue, masking tape
- three worlds descriptions copied and cut apart so each group will receive their tableau description (see Appendix D)
- digital camera (optional)
- sounds of chimes or other sounds or music to suggest an enchanted world (optional)
- props: scarf, hammer, crown (optional)

Overview: Scenes and Drama Strategies

SCENE 1   Creating Masks (art-making)
SCENE 2   Worlds Together (exploring characters)
SCENE 3   Three Worlds (**tableaux**, role play)
SCENE 4   Magic Potion (role play)
SCENE 5   Connecting Worlds (role play, **hot seat** adaptation)

Outline of the Role Drama

SCENE 1: *Creating Masks*

In advance, copy the mask cut-outs so that students will have one each (either cut for students or for them to cut for themselves) and prepare to present the dramatis personae, possibly by projecting it. (If you wish, revise the descriptions to suit your students.)

Write the character names on slips of paper using three different colours:

» one colour for the court of Athens—Theseus, Hippolyta, Egeus, Hermia, Lysander, Demetrius, Helena, and Philostrate
» one colour for the workers—Quince, Bottom, Flute, Snout, Snug, and Starveling
» one colour for the fairy world—Oberon, Titania, Puck, Peaseblossom, Cobweb, Moth, Mustardseed, and other fairies

Put the slips in a basket for students to choose from. As there are 22 character names, you might need to include some characters twice in order to have enough character names for your class size. (Alternatively, you could ask students to work in pairs to share a character.) Finally, gather markers, crayons, scissors, and other supplies to have them readily available.

As students enter the classroom, ask them each to choose a small slip of paper from a basket. *This is the character you will create a mask for.* Instruct them to use the displayed dramatis personae for reference. Ask students to visually illustrate on the mask the character they have chosen on the slip of paper; guide them to focus on colours, symbols, and facial features. Remind them that this is not a visual art class and their goal is to symbolically illustrate key features of the character rather than produce technically skilled artwork. You may show an example, or a series of examples, from another play to give them ideas on ways to visually create their character mask.

SCENE 2: *Worlds Together*

After students have completed their masks, explain that they will be joining groups and trying to identify the characters illustrated in the masks. Model how this can be done.

» *What do you see in this mask?*
» *What characteristics do you see represented?*

Examples of *Dream* character masks.

DISCOVERING SHAKESPEARE AND *A MIDSUMMER NIGHT'S DREAM*   49

Then ask students to form three small groups according to the colour of the paper strip they each have. (This will group students as members of the court of Athens, workers, and the fairy world.) Ask students to each show their masks in their groups without naming their characters and in turn ask the rest of the group to identify which character is illustrated on each mask. This encourages students to keep looking at the character list, which helps them become familiar with the various characters and be able to identify relationships. Emphasize first identifying the features represented on the mask and then trying to determine the character. Provide ample time for the three groups to share their masks in their groups. Invite students who wish to show their masks to the entire class to share their work. You might wish to explain to students the three worlds represented in *Dream* (fairy world, Athens court, and workers) and share insights about the distinction of the social classes. Referring back to the Athenian Market role drama will help depict the role of the villagers and the court.

SCENE 3: *Three Worlds*

Give each group a copy from the Three Worlds descriptions (see below). Guide each group to create a tableau to depict the moment or scene (below) from the play that represents their particular world. Note that each group should focus on creating a tableau where all members participate and make use of their character masks. The tableaux can move beyond the literal and explore possibilities other than the scenarios described.

A. FAIRY WORLD—squabbling over a child: *Oberon and Titania have an ongoing argument over who should care for a young human boy. Titania insists that the boy's mother was a friend of hers and so Titania should raise the child. Oberon likes the boy and jealously wants him as his servant. Titania refuses to part with the boy, and in frustration forbids Oberon's company altogether.*

B. WORKERS—rehearsing a play: *The workers are rehearsing a play. Led by their director, Quince, they will perform* The Most Lamentable Comedy, and Most Cruel Death of Pyramus and Thisby. *Bottom is supposed to play Pyramus, a man who kills himself for love. Flute will reluctantly play Thisby, the lady Pyramus must love. Starveling will undertake the role of Thisby's mother, while Snout plays Pyramus' father. Snug, despite his shyness, will play Lion, who only needs to roar.*

C. ATHENS COURT—hosting a wedding: *Three couples have just been married— Duke Theseus and Duchess Hippolyta, Hermia and Lysander, and Helena and Demetrius. Their ceremony is over and they walk towards family and friends to celebrate. Egeus and Philostrate welcome them in the garden.*

Once students have developed and rehearsed their tableaux, ask them to do a dress rehearsal. After the dress rehearsal, guide each group to share their work with the rest of the class, using the masks to assist them in their frozen images. If possible, take digital photos of the tableaux, as these images could be revisited later in the process of working on the play. Invite and guide students to comment or ask questions about the tableaux, if time permits.

SCENE 4: *Magic Potion*

Ask the groups to use the entire classroom space and simultaneously repeat their tableaux from the previous scene, staying frozen for a few moments. While they are frozen, and possibly while using the sounds of chimes or other music to suggest an enchanted world, take on the role of Puck to sprinkle magic potion onto the three tableaux: *This magic potion will affect your characters, and you might take on different actions. You might like someone you disliked, or dislike someone you liked. For instance, instead of arguing, Oberon and Titania might agree.*

Instruct the groups to unfreeze and brainstorm how the magic potion has changed their characters. Then each group can rehearse their new tableau. After they have been given sufficient time to brainstorm and rehearse their new tableau, ask each group to share the results: present their initial tableau and then—at your signal, as Puck sprinkling a potion—transform the outcome to their second tableau. You might ask the viewers to close their eyes while a group transitions into a second tableau, showing the effects of the magic potion. If time permits, ask students to comment on what they saw in one another's tableaux transformations.

SCENE 5: *Connecting Worlds*

Create a space on the floor in the centre of the room and divide it into three areas: fairy world, workers, and Athens court. If you wish, divide the space with masking tape and provide each area with an appropriate prop—for example, a silky scarf for the fairies, a plastic saw or hammer for the workers, and a crown for the court.

The following is an adapted hot seat activity where students take on a role and react and respond in that role. Instruct students to place their masks in the area where their character resides near the appropriate prop (i.e., Bottom's mask would go near the hammer) and then sit in a circle. Invite students to make predictions about how they think characters from one world might connect or intersect with another. You could give one of the following examples.

» Pick up the Oberon mask and take it over to the workers. In role as Oberon and holding an imaginary flower or potion, you could say: *With this spell I will give you some beautiful costumes so you will look fabulous in your play!*

> » Take Flute's mask and go over to the fairies: *I have to play a special role in a play. Can you give me a magical voice?*

Invite students to think of possible interactions among the three worlds. Remind them to stay in role as they intersect with other worlds. Assure them that no ideas are wrong and anything can happen in the dream world of the play.

At the end of the activity, it is important for you to place the students' masks on the wall. Label them with the character names on the front and student names on the back. The masks become visual reminders for students as they continue their study of the play.

Debriefing and Reflections

Continuing from where scene 5 left off, welcome any other questions or comments from students about connections and intersections between the worlds. Students can also comment and elaborate on their experience of creating masks and tableaux. They might comment on the transformation scene. *How did this role drama connect to previous ones we have done?*

You can introduce a writing/drawing activity in which students describe how the magic potion has the ability to change things. Prompt them to consider what they would do if they had the ability to sprinkle magic potion on something or someone. *What transformation would you wish to see?*

Curricular Objectives

This role drama aims to help students become familiar with the various characters and the three distinct worlds within *Dream*. Using a visual focus helps students use another part of their brains to represent their understanding of the written character descriptions. The activity also creates a community environment as students are creating the masks for the full list of characters in the play. Metaphorically, they are beginning to build *their* play, and this activity helps begin the ensemble focus of the work. Key literacy strands are also emphasized in this role drama as students read, visually respond, speak, listen, and communicate through gesture and voice in the sequence of activities. They are asked to make inferences about the characters throughout, and in the end they creatively seek to find connections between the various worlds of the play.

Extensions and Variations

A possible variation is to create simple puppets rather than masks, as one teacher comments (page 55).

After working on the play, the same drama-based activities with the masks could be used to revisit what students learned. For instance, what could be added to the *Dream* masks after exploring the play? What other layers have been discovered?

Now that they know more about these Shakespearean characters, ask students if the characters resemble other literary characters encountered in class, or outside of class. What new levels could be added to the initial tableaux created during the role drama among the characters? Digital photos of the initial tableaux can be shown to help remind students of their earlier work. Revisiting the initial drama work helps students recognize the journey they took, reviewing where they began and how far they have come, essentially marking their learning.

The mask-making activity can be used to introduce other plays or novels that have many characters. It may also be adapted into social studies units where a number of historical figures appear.

Assessment

Rather than focusing assessment on the level of artistry in creating the masks, examine ways in which students have used insightful symbols on their masks, colours for mood, or other methods that illustrate their understanding of a character. The tableaux and predicting activities invite creativity and use of the body to show learning. It is important to provide oral or written feedback to students about how they use space and physical expression with their bodies to show understanding. Commenting on their ability to transfer knowledge from one setting to another helps them understand that engaging in literacy activities is often about building and scaffolding our learning from one context and applying it to another.

For more about assessment, see Role Drama 1: Who Art Thou Shakespeare? (page 31).

> I liked how Jacqueline added wings to First Fairy!
> I liked the heart-shape eyes for Hermia on your mask.
> Who did you make? I made Puck, the nasty Fairy! I did Duke Theseus.
> Jack made Bottom, the silly guy. Part donkey.
> I want my parents to see our masks. Me too!
> —STUDENTS DURING A DEBRIEFING

> I used the mask role drama a few years in a row with different Shakespeare plays. I really find it useful as it allows the children to bring [forth] their understanding of the characters in a visual way. Also, creating the characters on masks provides the children an opportunity to learn how specific traits—such as dark, slightly slanted eyebrows for Oberon or Puck—might suggest mischievousness. This also brought forth how appearances can be

stereotyped, which invited valuable discussions about prejudice and how looks may not always speak to the truth of a character or person. Finally, and as importantly, the hung masks became a visual reminder of the play's characters. —TEACHER

Character masks help bring Shakespeare's characters to life.

Using different art forms supports the use of multi-literacies, which offers different entry points for learners (Anderson 2012; Belliveau and Prendergast 2013). Students who are visual learners are able to show their understanding through their images on the masks. This is also reinforced/encouraged throughout the Shakespeare-based research project as students are asked to visually represent their learning in their *Dream* journals. Reason (2010) has conducted extensive studies in the UK looking at children's visual responses to theatre. He has studied how children can illustrate their understanding through their images, and in turn how these visuals become starting points for them to discuss their understanding of a play. The visual work becomes an important outlet for children to share their understanding and make meaning. —RESEARCHER/OBSERVER

One year I decided to do small puppets instead of masks for this activity. I brought in different fabrics and the students cut them to create costumes for their characters. This adaptation worked really well, although the cutting of material took much longer than anticipated! —TEACHER

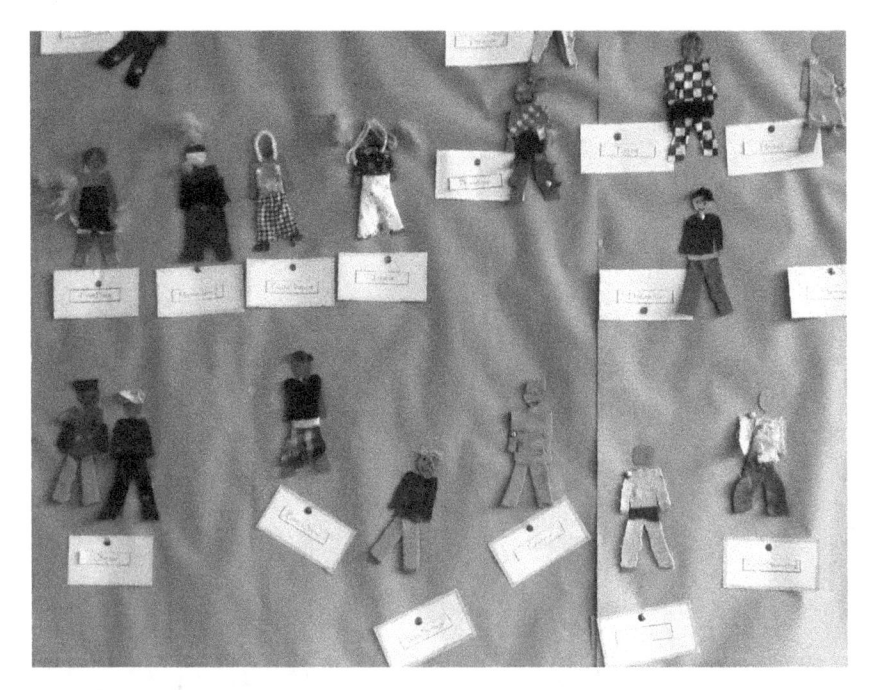

Puppets created by children for *Dream*.

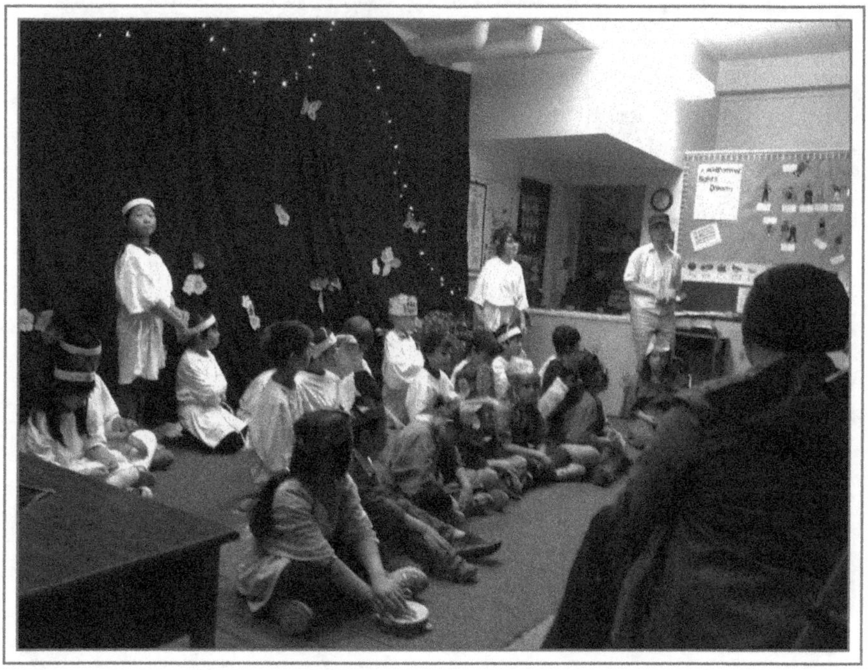

PART III

ENGAGING WITH THE STORY OF *A MIDSUMMER NIGHT'S DREAM*

THE EIGHT DRAMA-BASED LESSONS IN THIS PART ARE DESIGNED TO guide students through *Dream* in the form of an abridged story in eight parts. Each lesson offers a short narrative that recounts a major event in the play along with specific drama activities building on that section of the story. The brief narratives are meant to introduce the story, the characters, and key issues that arise in the play. The eight lessons are intended to be explored in sequence.

The following table provides an overview of the lessons and where the corresponding portion of the play can be found.

LESSONS FOR THE STORY ADAPTATION	PLAY
1. Mighty Law of Athens and Runaway Plan (page 60)	pages 128–133
2. A Play for Theseus' Wedding Day (page 66)	pages 134–138
3. Titania and Oberon Clash (page 71)	pages 139–144
4. Spells Are Everywhere in the Wood (page 76)	pages 144–147
5. Puck Plays in Devilish Ways (page 81)	pages 147–156
6. Lovers' Quarrel (page 87)	pages 157–166
7. Release of Spells and All Is Well (page 92)	pages 166–172
8. Play Within the Play on Wedding Day (page 97)	pages 172–180

USING THE STORY VERSION AND LESSONS

The complete narrative of the play appears in both the lessons that follow in this part and in Appendix E. Note:

» Each of the eight lessons lasts 45 to 75 minutes, depending on how much time you wish to spend on each activity. Suggested times are included for each activity.
» An open space with room to move around is preferred for both the warm-up and drama-based activities.

- » A variety of drama strategies are introduced in this section. Some drama strategies (highlighted in boldface because they are glossary terms) are also described in Appendix A.
- » How much writing and illustrating you ask your students to do will depend on their age, the time available, and your curricular goals. The writing students undertake in their journals may be adapted into a class newspaper or theatre program. Samples of student writing and drawing appear throughout this section.
- » You will also find many comments from teachers, students, and researchers/observers in this part, as in earlier sections.
- » To address vocabulary, creating a student word wall is effective. For each lesson and to create a word wall, you will find handy definitions that are adapted to be appropriate for the ages of students. The words are defined in the order in which they appear in the story version and are highlighted in the story excerpt. Based on student needs and interests, you might revise the word lists as you see fit.
- » As with Part II, you will find suggested teacher scripts to provide instructions during the eight lessons. You may adapt and expand these as needed for your purposes.

For each of the eight lessons, you will find the following in this part:

- » notes about materials, focus, and suggested times
- » warm-up activities
- » vocabulary words and their definitions
- » suggestions for reading the portion of the adapted story
- » the story portion itself
- » additional activities
- » debriefing and journal reflections

> I have seen reserved students, those who do not read or write well, and of course the most boisterous children engage dynamically when drama activities have been part of their learning. I have seen children engaged, motivated, and enthusiastic, relating to the text in a much more meaningful way than if I was only to do a read aloud or [give] a regular lesson. I have witnessed firsthand—from the shyest to the troublesome to the academically challenged—how all children have had an equal chance to be triumphant in their learning when I use drama in my lessons. —TEACHER

LESSON 1:
MIGHTY LAW OF ATHENS AND RUNAWAY PLAN

1. Warm-up activities

- » **MATERIALS:** none
- » **FOCUS:** build community and explore movement
- » **SUGGESTED TIME:** 5 minutes for each warm-up activity

GREETING GAME. Using the entire space of the classroom, ask students to walk freely and try to fill any open area within the classroom with their bodies.

> *Keep moving and find the empty spaces. No talking. Just walk and be aware of the open spaces."*

Continue this activity for a minute or so.

> *Keep walking in the open space, but when you encounter another student, say 'hello' with a wink of your eye."*

Continue for 30 seconds.

> *Keep walking and now touch pinkies with other students that you encounter ... then touch elbows."*

You can suggest variations such as toes, hips, and so on

> *... and STOP!"*

I repeat these activities early in the year. It helps students to control their bodies and to take direction. —TEACHER

GROUPS AND TABLEAUX. Have students walk in the open space once again, finding empty spaces. Continue for 10–15 seconds.

> *Now, without talking, form groups of two and stand still."*

If there is an uneven number in the class, having one group of three is fine.

> "*Release yourself from the group and begin walking in the space again. Now form groups of three and be still. Release and form groups of four. Release and form groups of five. Release. For the final group, form groups of two. Now, in your group of two create a frozen image, a **tableau** of a king and a queen.*"

Give students a minute or two to work out their tableaux. Then, count them down to their frozen image:

> "*5, 4, 3, 2, 1 and freeze in your tableau of a king and queen. Stay frozen for a moment. Release the image. With the same partner, create a tableau of a happy father and daughter.*"

Count down again:

> "*5, 4, 3, 2, 1 and freeze, and stay frozen in your tableau of a happy father and daughter.*"

Now ask students to reverse roles.

> "*The father becomes the daughter and the daughter becomes the father, and you are now an unhappy father and daughter. Create this tableau ... and freeze. Release.*"

If time permits, **debrief** students about the warm-up activities by asking them to briefly share their experiences.

> » MATERIALS: cue cards, word wall
>
> » FOCUS: build understanding and vocabulary
>
> » SUGGESTED TIME: 10 minutes

2. Introduce vocabulary

> **Duke**—*noun*—the ruler of a territory, a member of the nobility
> **irate**—*adjective*—angry, enraged, upset
> **vexation**—*noun*—anger, frustration, annoyance
> **refuse**—*verb*—to be unwilling to do something, reject, or say "no"
> **nun**—*noun*—a woman belonging to a religious community and following certain rules, such as a Catholic nun
> **devise**—*verb*—to imagine, organize, or plan

The words are taken from the story portion and defined. Prepare cue cards for the vocabulary and share the words one at a time.

For each word, display the word, read it, and explain its meaning. Have students repeat the word with you a few times. Then, looking closely at the word, discuss its spelling.

> " *Are there some root words within this word? Do you notice anything about the beginning or ending of the word? Is the word a noun, adjective, verb, or adverb?"*

After a brief discussion of each word, ask a student to place the cue card on the word wall.

An example of a word wall.

STEPPING INTO DRAMA

3. Read the adapted story

Point to words on the word wall as they appear in the story. This will help put the words into context and reinforce their meaning. You may also stop to discuss key issues faced by the characters in the narrative. Alternatively, you might wish to read aloud the entire narrative and then discuss the story.

> **MATERIALS:** story (Appendix E)
>
> **FOCUS:** listen and respond
>
> **SUGGESTED TIME:** 15 minutes

Mighty Law of Athens and Runaway Plan

Excitement is growing throughout Athens and its surroundings because, in four days, **Duke** Theseus will marry Queen Hippolyta. Inside the Duke's palace, attendants and servants are busily preparing for the celebration. However, the merriments are abruptly put aside when Egeus barges in to see the Duke. Egeus, an **irate** father, says: "Full of **vexation** come I, against my daughter Hermia." Egeus has promised her to marry Demetrius, the young Athenian, but Hermia is strong-willed and **refuses.** She wishes to marry Lysander instead. In a kind but firm manner, Duke Theseus reminds Hermia of the Athenian law that allows fathers to choose their daughters' husbands; if not, they must die or become **nuns** and so never marry.

Left with little choice, Hermia and Lysander **devise** an escape plan to a nearby village where Athenian law does not rule. First they will meet in a nearby wood at dusk, and then they will make their way together to the village. Prior to leaving Athens, Hermia confides in her best friend, Helena, telling her the plan. However, the problem is that Helena loves Demetrius and she wants desperately to win his love. Helena decides to tell Demetrius about the escape plan. She thinks Demetrius will want to pursue Hermia, and Helena plans to follow also. As night falls, one by one, the four young Athenians leave the safety of the city to enter the spirit-filled wood outside of Athens.

Here are some suggested discussion questions:

» *What do you think of the Athenian Law that allows fathers to choose who their daughters will marry?*
» *What have we discovered about the friendship and loyalty between Hermia and Helena?*
» *Do you think the four young Athenians fear leaving the security of home, family, and friends? Would you?*

> Oh, that's why we froze like an angry Dad and his daughter!
> —STUDENT

- **MATERIALS:** chair or stool
- **FOCUS:** think in role, question
- **SUGGESTED TIME:** 15 minutes

4. Seek further information: Hot seating

HOT SEATING. This section of the story has provided information about the characters. Through putting someone in the **hot seat**, you can ask students to make further inferences about the characters. Begin with the irate father, Egeus. Ask for a volunteer to role play Egeus in the hot seat. Don't let gender limit the students; remind them that boys can role play daughters and girls can role play fathers during hot seating. Ask the rest of the class to put on their thinking caps and consider questions they could ask Egeus to help them better understand his motives. Several students may have similar questions, which means these are important questions, but it is not necessary to repeat them.

Here are a few suggested questions for Egeus if students don't come up with any:

> I was really nervus in the hot seat but then it was fun. I like making up the carackters. —STUDENT

» Have you spoken to Hermia about her feelings towards Demetrius?
» Did you know about Hermia and Lysander's relationship?
» Would you like your daughter to be happy?

Next, hot seat Hermia, asking students:

» Are there any volunteers to be Hermia?
» What questions do you have for Hermia?

Here are a few suggested questions for Hermia:

» Are you afraid of leaving Athens?
» What might you miss about home and family?

For a final hot seat, ask Helena questions.

> "Any volunteers to be Helena? What questions do you have for Helena?"

Here are a few suggested questions for Helena:

» Should you have told Demetrius about Hermia and Lysander's secret?
» Will you miss Hermia if she runs away?
» Are you afraid of going in the wood?

STEPPING INTO DRAMA

5. Debriefing and journal reflections

Begin **debriefing** the lesson by asking students what they discovered in the activities.

> *"Were there any surprises? Does anyone want to share their experience?"*

Suggest that students retell parts of what they heard in today's section of the story in their dream journals. Have them begin by drawing a picture of something they remember from the story or one of the activities. Ask students to write a few sentences explaining their picture or something they remember from today's reading. Suggest that they try to use words from the word wall.

> *"Try to use at least two or three words from the vocabulary that was added to the word wall today."*

» **MATERIALS:** dream journal

» **FOCUS:** write/draw and respond

» **SUGGESTED TIME:** 15 minutes

It's important to spend time debriefing. After the warm-up, I ask students, *"Why do you think we did tableaux of kings and queens, fathers and daughters?"* I want them to engage in predictions. They usually tell me about other stories they know with kings and queens. —TEACHER

I find I need to prepare my students for hot seating. I sometimes ask them to brainstorm with a partner questions they could ask a character. I also find it helpful to model a few questions to get them started. —TEACHER

Egeus is upset with his daughter Hermia.

LESSON 2:
A PLAY FOR THESEUS' WEDDING DAY

1. Warm-up activities

- » **MATERIALS:** none
- » **FOCUS:** build community, ensemble work
- » **SUGGESTED TIME:** 5 minutes for each warm-up

I use this activity often as it reinforces giving and receiving ideas. It becomes a key warm-up during rehearsals. The younger students find it challenging initially, so scaffolding (and patience) is needed.
—TEACHER

PASS THE ENERGY. Ask students to stand in a large circle in the centre of the room and **pass the energy**.

❝*In a moment, I will begin by turning to the person on my right and sending a clap.*❞

Say to the person on your right:

❝*You will turn to the person on your right and clap your hands. The person on that person's right then turns to the next person on the right and claps at that person. This 'passing' of a clap represents passing our energy around a circle.*❞

Continue around the circle a few times. Once students are comfortable with passing the energy around the circle, stop the clapping. Next, do the same thing, except when you turn to your right, the person beside you will clap at the same time as you.

❝*Using eye contact and signalling with your hands helps you get in sync with the person beside you, as it signals being ready to clap. The person beside you then turns to the next person ... and they clap their hands at the same time. This person then turns to the next ... they clap their hands together, until it goes all around the circle.*❞

Allow the group to go around the circle a few times so they get the flow of the activity.

❝*Now, let's change directions.*❞

Go around the circle beginning to your left, with the same idea of clapping together when you turn to your partner beside you.

SHAPES AND NUMBERS. Ask students to walk freely, using the entire space of the classroom, and try to **fill in the space**, filling any open area with their bodies.

> *Keep moving and find the empty spaces. No talking, just walking and being aware of the open spaces."*

Keep the activity going for 15–20 seconds.

> *Now, without talking, form groups of two and stand still."*

If there's an uneven number in the class there will be one group of three.

> *Now, walk again in the space, and form groups of three and stand still... Form groups of four."*

> *Keep walking. Now, imagine a helicopter is in the air and a photographer wants to take a picture ... of a square. Without talking, form a square with your bodies."*

Once they accomplish their square, take an imaginary photo with optional vocal sound effects.

> *Release your square, and begin walking again. Now, the photographer wants to take another picture, this time of two circles side by side... make the circles only using your bodies...."*

Allow time for students to complete circles. Take the photo.

> *Wow, this looked like an 8. Release the two circles and walk. Now create one large triangle. Release.... Now one large X...."*

If time permits, **debrief** the students about the warm-up activities by asking them to briefly share their experiences.

I have used this activity with my students to reinforce letters and numbers as well as shapes for geometry, integrating parts of the math curriculum. —TEACHER

---

2. Introduce vocabulary

- » **MATERIALS:** cue cards, word wall
- » **FOCUS:** build understanding and vocabulary
- » **SUGGESTED TIME:** 10 minutes

> **lamentable**—*adjective*—sad, regrettable, unfortunate, or possibly horribly bad
> **amateur**—*adjective*—inexperienced or unpolished in performance; doing something for the love of it rather than for pay
> **bombastic**—*adjective*—pompous or extravagant
> **gallant**—*adverb*—bravely and nobly; attentive, especially in love
> **scroll**—*noun*—a roll of paper to be read, with the lines for the actor

The words are taken from the story portion and defined. Prepare cue cards for the vocabulary and share the words one at a time. Use the same approach as in Lesson 1 (page 62).

3. Read the adapted story

- » **MATERIALS:** story (Appendix E)
- » **FOCUS:** listen and respond
- » **SUGGESTED TIME:** 15 minutes

You might begin by asking your students what occurred in the story in the previous lesson, and reviewing with them key moments and characters that were introduced.

See Lesson 1 (page 63) for ideas and suggestions on ways to introduce the story portion with your class.

A Play for Theseus' Wedding Day!

A group of local workers has gathered near Athens to rehearse a play in hopes of performing it at the upcoming wedding celebrations of the Duke. The play is *The Most **Lamentable** Comedy, and Most Cruel Death of Pyramus and Thisby*. Led by their director Peter Quince, a carpenter, the budding **amateur** actors begin casting the play. A weaver named Nick Bottom is the most **bombastic** of the group and is slated to play Pyramus, a lover who kills himself most **gallant** for love. Francis Flute the bellows-mender will reluctantly play Thisby, the lady Pyramus loves. Robin Starveling the tailor will play Thisby's mother; while Tom Snout the tinker must play Pyramus' father. Finally, Snug the joiner will play the ferocious Lion, who only needs to roar. Despite his shyness and worry about memorizing lines, he accepts his role.

The very confident Bottom tells Quince that he could undertake the parts of Thisby and Lion as well. Quince firmly responds that Bottom "can play no part but Pyramus!" With excitement and fear, the troupe of amateurs set out to memorize their lines from the **scroll** by tomorrow night, when they will rehearse in the wood near Athens.

Here are some suggested discussion questions:

» *Why do you think these workers want to be part of a play production?*
» *Based on what you know from the story, do you think their play will be well received?*
» *What do we learn about Bottom and the other actors in this scene?*

4. Director, actor, sculptors—a lover that kills himself most gallant for love

SCULPTING A TABLEAU. The story in today's lesson provides key information about the actors and Quince as their director. Group students in pairs so that Quince will be **sculpting** Bottom to create a **tableau**:

> *In your pairs, one of you will be Quince and the other Bottom. Quince, as the director, must 'shape' the actor into 'a lover, that kills himself most gallant for love.' In other words, like a sculptor with a lump of clay, Quince must gently shape and refine how Bottom presents himself. Quince, you are to guide your partner gently and with respect for your partner's body to form a tableau of a young man in love, noble and brave. Bottom, you are to follow your partner's guidance with care and respecting your partner's body to create a tableau of Bottom in the role of Pyramus."*

Give pairs one or two minutes to sculpt/guide their artwork.

> *Now, switch roles, so that the first Quince becomes Bottom and vice versa, and begin sculpting."*

If time permits, you can walk through an imagined gallery where frozen sculptures (tableaux of students as Bottom in role as Pyramus) are viewed by the sculptors (Quinces) walking around the space. Then, switch to see the second set of frozen sculptures.

» **MATERIALS:** Shakespeare line on the board or projected
» **FOCUS:** depict character through the body
» **SUGGESTED TIME:** 10 minutes

I like the character Nick Bottom. He's funny and he wants to do all the jobs.
—STUDENT

- **MATERIALS:** dream journal
- **FOCUS:** write/draw and respond
- **SUGGESTED TIME:** 15 minutes

5. Debriefing and journal reflections

See Lesson 1 (page 65) for suggestions on ways of inviting students to **debrief** orally and reflect in their writing journals.

For their journal response in this lesson, students might draw a picture of their sculpture of Bottom.

I often used the leaves and flowers to have my students make a brief comment about how they felt at the end of a lesson. Their comments then became part of our set! These reflections on the leaves and flowers gave them a break from writing in their journals. —TEACHER

I found doing a checking-in circle at the beginning of these lessons beneficial. It only took about five minutes or less but it was well worth the time. Sometimes I only had time for one word or so from each child, checking in where they were, "taking the temperature." Giving children the opportunity to let me know where they were [and] how they were feeling prior to us beginning the drama work was important. Sometimes, I was able to do a quick check-out after our debriefing and before I let them write in their journals. —TEACHER

Student comments about the drama activities written on leaves and flowers.

Integrating Shakespeare's language early in the process is important as it familiarizes the students to some of the inversions, poetry, and turns of phrase in the plays. The students also enjoy speaking the heightened language, as it helps them role play the various characters (Winston and Tandy 2012). The sculpting activity (Boal 2002) introduces students to trust-building as they shape one another's body. Showing meaning through body representations immerses them into the non-verbal communication side of drama learning (Culham 2002). —RESEARCHER/OBSERVER

LESSON 3:
TITANIA AND OBERON CLASH

1. Warm-up activities

GROUPS AND TABLEAUX. Have students begin by walking about in the space. They try to find the empty spaces. Give them 15–20 seconds.

> *"Now, without talking, form groups of two and stand still."*

If there is an uneven number of students in the class, you can create one group of three.

> *"Now, walk again in the space, and form groups of three and stand still…."*

> *"Walk again, and now form groups of four…. Walk in the space again, and form groups of two and stand still."*

> *"Pause. In this group of two, create a frozen image, a tableau of two people fighting over the same object."*

Give students 10–15 seconds.

> *"Stay frozen for a moment, and release the image. With the same partner, I want you to create a frozen image of someone putting a spell on another person."*

Give them 10–15 seconds.

> *"Release. I want you now to move around the space as if you were a magical spirit, like Peter Pan, flying around. Now gently slow down, and you're putting a spell on something in the far distance. And freeze just as you cast your spell…. And release."*

Pause.

- » **MATERIALS:** none
- » **FOCUS:** build community and develop characters
- » **SUGGESTED TIME:** 5 minutes

> "*Walk around the space again. You now feel very tired. You've been walking for hours and you feel quite lost and tired. Slowly and gently find a place on the ground where you will sleep. And when you are ready, freeze into a sleeping position.*"

If time permits, debrief students about the warm-up activities by asking them to briefly share their experiences.

> I remind students not to always work with the same partner. I try to find ways to mix up the pairs. —TEACHER

- » **MATERIALS:** cue cards, word wall
- » **FOCUS:** build understanding and vocabulary
- » **SUGGESTED TIME:** 10 minutes

2. Introduce vocabulary

> **quarrel**—*noun*—an argument, dispute, or fight
> **forbid**—*verb*—to refuse to allow, to order someone not to do something
> **anoint**—*verb*—to apply or rub with something, such as drops of medicine

The words are taken from the story portion and defined. Prepare cue cards for the vocabulary and share the words one at a time. Use the same approach as in Lesson 1 (page 62).

- » **MATERIALS:** story (Appendix E)
- » **FOCUS:** listen and respond
- » **SUGGESTED TIME:** 15 minutes

3. Read the adapted story

You might begin by asking your students what occurred in the story in the previous lesson, and then review with them key moments and characters that were introduced.

See Lesson 1 (page 63) for ideas and suggestions on ways to introduce the story portion with your class.

Titania and Oberon Clash

Meanwhile, in another part of the wood, Oberon, King of the Fairies, and Titania, Queen of the Fairies, continue a **quarrel** over who should care for a young human boy. Titania insists that the boy's mother, who died in childbirth, was a friend: "And for her sake do I rear him up. And I will not part with him!" Oberon is jealous and wants the boy to be his servant. Titania refuses to part with the boy, and in frustration, **forbids** Oberon's company altogether. To seek revenge, Oberon directs his servant, Puck, to squeeze the juice of a special herb into Titania's eyes while she sleeps so that when she wakes, she will fall in love with the first thing she sees, whether it is a lion, bear, wolf, or bull "she shall pursue it with the soul of love!"

While plotting their trick on Titania, Puck and Oberon overhear two of the escaped Athenians, Demetrius and Helena. Helena is deeply in love with Demetrius, but he rudely refuses her. Oberon feels sad for Helena and tries to help the pair. He commands Puck to **anoint** the young man (Demetrius) with a love potion when he is asleep so that Demetrius will instantly fall in love with the first person he sees when he awakes—Helena!

Here are some suggested discussion questions:

» *What would you propose to Titania and Oberon to help resolve their quarrel?*
» *What do you think of the trick Oberon and Puck plan to play on Titania?*
» *What might happen when the human world and the world of the fairies meet? What conflicts might take place?*

4. Seek further information

GROUP HOT SEATING. This portion of the story has given us insights into the fairy or spirit characters. The activity helps students uncover more details about the motives and histories of these characters.

> My students preferred the group hot seating to individual hot seats. With three Titanias on the hot seat, the activity seemed to be full of energy and varied responses. —TEACHER

Invite up to three students who would like to role play Oberon in the hot seat. Once there are volunteers, ask the other students to think of questions they could ask Oberon to help further understand why he wants the human boy.

❝ *We will build on the hot seating we explored during Lesson 1, but this time we will have more than one person in the hot seat. We'll*

» **MATERIALS:** none

» **FOCUS:** think, question in role, and respond collectively

» **SUGGESTED TIME:** 15 minutes

have three Oberons to ask questions of and they might each have different perspectives."

Have the other students brainstorm questions for Oberon. If no one comes up with questions to begin, here are a few suggestions to ask the Oberons:

» *Have you and Titania talked about ways of sharing the human boy?*
» *Have you asked the human boy what he might want?*

Ask for up to three students to volunteer to be in the hot seat for Titania. The following are suggested questions for the Titanias:

» *What was your relationship with the human boy's mother?*
» *Were you friends for a long time?*
» *How did you know her? Do you miss her?*
» *Have you talked to Oberon about ways to settle the quarrel?*

And, finally, add a group hot seat for the human boy. If needed, suggest questions for the human boys:

» *Who do you like spending time with? Why?*
» *What do you think of the world of the fairies and the forest?*
» *Do you miss home?*

I liked the human boy in the hot seat becus we cood invent his character. His mum lovd him but died of fever. His dad was in a soldier war so gon. —STUDENT

---

5. Debriefing and journal reflections

See Lesson 1 (page 65) for suggested ways of inviting students to **debrief** orally and reflect in their writing journals.

» **MATERIALS:** dream journal

» **FOCUS:** write/draw and respond

» **SUGGESTED TIME:** 15 minutes

In many ways, the drama activities become character preparation for students prior to their class production. Critically thinking about character motives through hot seating allows the whole class to have input and co-create the respective characters. Come production time, the students who interpret roles such as Titania and Oberon have a deeper understanding of the possible motives their character has within the play. Group hot seating, one of many hot seating variations (Even 2011; Wilhelm 2002), helps illustrate the complexity of Shakespeare's characters and at the same time human traits such as jealousy, greed, love that are familiar to people of all ages (Doona 2012). —RESEARCHER/OBSERVER

The King and Queen of the Fairies, fighting over the human boy.

ENGAGING WITH THE STORY OF *A MIDSUMMER NIGHT'S DREAM*

LESSON 4:
SPELLS ARE EVERYWHERE IN THE WOOD

- » **MATERIALS:** chime (or other) musical sound effect
- » **FOCUS:** explore character walks, moods
- » **SUGGESTED TIME:** 3–5 minutes for each warm-up activity

1. Warm-up activities

MOODS. Ask students to walk in the space and try to find the empty spaces. Continue for 10–15 seconds.

> *"Without talking, walk as if you're very happy—light on your feet."*

Have students walk as though in different moods for 10–15 seconds.

> *"Now, you're really angry, walking with determination.
> Now walk as if you're very nervous, scared, afraid.
> And freeze.
> Now you're very tired, almost falling asleep as you walk."*

Our teacher remindid us often not to youse only our face but also our arms, shulders to show happy and sad emotions. —STUDENT

TRANSITIONS. Ask half the class to form a line and become group A and the other half of the class to form a second line to become group B. Ask groups A and B to face each other and stand approximately three or four metres apart.

> *"Group A: you are very happy; all is well with you. Group B: you are unhappy; everything is going wrong, woeful. When I say 'Begin walking,' both groups walk towards one another <u>very slowly</u>. Now begin walking."*

As the happy (group A) people and the unhappy (group B) people walk towards the centre of the space, sound the chime or other musical sound to illustrate the following:

> *"When you hear this sound, I want you to gradually change to the opposite mood."*

STEPPING INTO DRAMA

When the groups meet at the centre, make the sound.

> *Group A, you are now unhappy, and group B, happy. Continue to slowly walk in the same direction as when you started walking."*

Group A should end up where group B began and group B where group A began.

Repeat once, so that group A now begins unhappy and group B, happy. When the groups meet halfway, again make the chime or other musical sound. With that sound, students should change moods and walk in their transformed mood to the opposite side, from where they began.

If time permits, **debrief** students about the warm-up activities by asking them to briefly share their experiences.

Doing non-speaking activities initially seemed bizarre as I was preparing my class to do a Shakespeare play. However, I value the focus on body and movement to build characters … and I appreciate the silence! —TEACHER

---

2. Introduce vocabulary

mischievously—*adverb*—in a playful, teasing, troublesome manner, such as when pulling a prank
demoralized—*adjective*—made to feel hopeless or without confidence
pursuit—*noun*—the act of chasing, following
distraught—*adjective*—very upset, worried, fearful, or agitated

» **MATERIALS:** cue cards, word wall

» **FOCUS:** build understanding and vocabulary

» **SUGGESTED TIME:** 10 minutes

The words are taken from the story portion and defined. Prepare cue cards for the vocabulary and share the words one at a time. Use the same approach as in Lesson 1 (page 62). Additionally, you might point out the phrase "change a raven for a dove" and ask students what they know about these birds. *How do the birds compare? What comparison is Lysander making?*

> **MATERIALS:** story (Appendix E)
>
> **FOCUS:** listen and respond
>
> **SUGGESTED TIME:** 10 minutes

3. Read the adapted story

You might begin by asking your students what occurred in the story in the previous lesson, and reviewing with them key moments and characters that were introduced.

See Lesson 1 (page 63) for ideas and suggestions on ways to introduce this story portion to your class.

Spells Everywhere in the Wood

After Titania is lulled to sleep with songs by her fairies, Oberon **mischievously** sneaks in and pours the love juice on the sleeping Queen's eyelids. When she wakes she will fall madly in love with the first thing she sees.

Nearby in the wood, Lysander and Hermia are exhausted from walking and so lie down and sleep. Puck comes upon them sleeping and believes the young Athenian (Lysander) to be the man Oberon had directed him to (Demetrius). As per Oberon's orders, Puck nimbly anoints the eyes of the man (Lysander) with love juice, so that he will fall in love with the next person he sees when he awakes.

Within moments, Demetrius and Helena enter the same part of the wood. Demetrius is rude and unloving to Helena. He continues, but Helena stops and sits, **demoralized**. Soon, Helena notices that immediately beside her is Lysander. Is he dead or asleep, she wonders, and quickly wakes him. With the new love juice in his eyes, Lysander instantly falls in love with Helena (rather than Hermia).

> HELENA: Do not say so, Lysander; Hermia still loves you.
> LYSANDER: It's not Hermia but Helena I love:
> Who will not change a raven for a dove?

Helena cannot understand Lysander's change of heart and thinks he's making fun of her. She runs away, with Lysander in **pursuit**, which leaves Hermia asleep. Soon Hermia wakes up, alone and **distraught**, wondering where Lysander has gone.

Here are some suggested discussion questions to engage students with the story:

» *Who do you think Titania will see when she awakes? Do you think this was mean of Oberon or playful? Was it misunderstanding or mischievousness?*
» *Oberon tells Puck to anoint the young Athenian man by saying that Puck will know him by the Athenian clothes he has on. Do you think Puck was innocent in his mistake? Or was he being mischievous?*

4. Transform—Who will not change a raven for a dove?

TRANSFORM. Have students stand or sit in a large circle to play the **scarf game**. Place a scarf in the middle of the floor. Demonstrate how the scarf can be transformed into something different. For example, carefully pick up the scarf and roll it up, caress it, and rock it back and forth as if it were a baby. Or you could scrunch the scarf into a roundish object and mime bouncing it as if it were a ball. Ask student volunteers to transform the scarf into something different. It is important that, after students have finished showing the scarf transformed (to a baby, ball, and so on), they place the scarf back in the centre of the circle. This signifies that it is now neutral and can be transformed into something new by another student. After students do a few example transformations in the large class circle, divide your students into four groups to make four smaller circles. Place a scarf in the centre of each small circle and ask students to take turns transforming the scarf and then returning it to neutral in the centre, so someone else can have a turn.

» **MATERIALS:** 16–20 scarves (or pieces of loose fabric)
» **FOCUS:** imagination
» **SUGGESTED TIME:** 15 minutes

My students wanted to keep playing forever once their imagination was freed from what is right and wrong. —TEACHER

TRANSPORT. For this next activity, maintain the same four groups that participated in the activity above, and give each group at least 3–4 more scarves or pieces of cloth. The idea is to build belief and develop co-operative group work by transforming scarves and/or fabric into an imagined transportable but large object. If you wish, you might write some suggestions for possible objects on slips of paper—for example, a trampoline, dining table, piano, large mirror, bed, canoe. Ask each group to imagine and create a large object from a few scarves or pieces of fabric.

Then ask them to work as a group to take this imagined object from one place in the classroom to another. *What is your object? How will you lift and carry it? How will you use it?* Guide students to be very precise in the way they pick up their object, transport it, and eventually use it. For example, students might tie a few scarves and/or pieces of fabric together to bring to life a "canoe" and then **mime** picking up the canoe, carrying it to the water, and then sitting inside before paddling away.

> We carried a trampoleen then jumped on it! Kool! —STUDENT

5. Debriefing and journal reflections

> » **MATERIALS:** dream journal
>
> » **FOCUS:** write/draw and respond
>
> » **SUGGESTED TIME:** 15 minutes

See Lesson 1 (page 65) for suggested ways of inviting students to **debrief** orally and reflect in their writing journals. Students might share something about the imaginary objects they created or what they experienced in the mood transition activity.

> In our debriefing today, many of the students made the connection between the magical world of the fairies in the wood and our scarf changing into many objects. They talked about the scarf being magical like Puck and the fairies. The activity freed their imaginations and made links to the spirit world. —TEACHER

> *Dream* is one of Shakespeare's plays where the actors and audience have to believe in the "as if" imaginary world. Characters are put under spells and immediately fall in love with someone else. The suspension of disbelief has to be present for the audience. And this can only happen through the conviction of the actors, portraying how Titania dotes upon and deeply loves the donkey-headed Bottom, for instance. The transforming activity pushes students to be convincing with their actions and imaginative with their minds (Booth 2005; Miller and Saxton 2004). Taking on these small roles in the drama activities develops their drama muscles and skills, warming the students up for future collaborative and creative work. —RESEARCHER/OBSERVER

STEPPING INTO DRAMA

LESSON 5:
PUCK PLAYS IN DEVILISH WAYS

1. Warm-up activities

WHAT ARE YOU DOING? Building on last lesson's transformation of objects, this activity guides students to **mime** doing one activity while stating they are doing something different. Have students form a large circle. Ask for a volunteer to go to the centre of the circle and perform an action. For instance, the student mimes brushing his or her teeth. Have another student enter the circle and ask:

> "Hey, what are you doing?"

The student brushing his or her teeth might say:

> "Oh, I'm washing my dog!"

The new person who entered the circle then begins washing an imaginary dog, while the person who was brushing his or her teeth goes back to the outer circle with the rest of the class. A new person enters the playing space inside the circle, and asks the person who is continuing to wash the dog:

> "Hey, what are you doing?"

The student washing the dog might say:

> "Oh, I'm skipping with my new rope!"

The new person begins to skip, and the activity continues.
  Guide students so that they repeat the pattern: one student mimes an action, another asks what the student is doing, and the mime says something that contradicts his or her action.
  Once students get used to the activity, you might divide the class into two groups so there is less waiting and more doing.
  If time permits, **debrief** students about the warm-up activity by asking them to briefly share their experiences.

> » **MATERIALS:** none
>
> » **FOCUS:** voice and body
>
> » **SUGGESTED TIME:** 10 minutes

> I needed to repeat the instructions a few times, but once they got it, they loved it! With my younger students, it was useful to brainstorm a few actions and put them on the board. —TEACHER
>
> I love this game. Sara and I playd it at recess with girls in the other class. We change the rules. —STUDENT

Puck puts spells on Athenians.

2. Introduce vocabulary

- » **MATERIALS:** cue cards, word wall
- » **FOCUS:** build understanding and vocabulary
- » **SUGGESTED TIME:** 10 minutes

> **chink**—*noun*—a crack, slit, or small hole in a wall
> **hempen home-spuns**—*noun*—common folk; referring to their poor, homemade clothing
> **nozzle**—*noun*—spout or, in this case, the muzzle
> **bower**—*noun*—a private shelter or retreat, such as in a garden
> **hoarse**—*adjective*—rough, harsh sounding

The words are taken from the story portion and defined. Prepare cue cards for the vocabulary and share the words one at a time. Use the same approach as in Lesson 1 (page 62).

3. Read the adapted story

You might begin by asking your students what occurred in the story in the previous lesson, and review with them key moments and characters so far. See Lesson 1 (page 63) for ideas and suggestions on ways to introduce the story portion to your class.

> » **MATERIALS:** story (Appendix E)
> » **FOCUS:** listen and respond
> » **SUGGESTED TIME:** 10 minutes

Puck Plays in Devilish Ways

In another part of the wood, the amateur actors are busily rehearsing their play and trying to resolve some of the acting challenges. They decide that it would be best to explain to their audience that no one gets hurt in the play and the lion is not real. They also agree to have Starveling play the moon because the moon shines the night Pyramus and Thisby meet. Last, they decide to have Snout play a wall because Pyramus and Thisby talk through a **chink** in a wall. Finally, they can rehearse!

Puck observes these **hempen home-spuns** and thinks it would be quite fun to have Titania fall in love with Bottom. Using his magical powers, Puck leads Bottom into a clearing within the wood and changes his head to a donkey's head. Unaware of his new appearance, Bottom terrifies his fellow actors with his animal ears and **nozzle**. The others run away screaming, leaving Bottom singing away with his donkey head. He approaches Titania's **bower** and wakens her. She instantly falls in love with his **hoarse** voice and long ears! He joins Queen Titania inside the bower and she commands her fairies to:

> *Feed him with apricots and dewberries,*
> *With purple grapes, green figs, and mulberries.*

The mismatched couple are as happy as can be, much to Puck's sneaky delight!

Here are some suggested discussion questions:

- » *How did the workers creatively resolve their staging challenges? What do you think of their ideas?*
- » *In your opinion, what does Puck think of these actors?*
- » *Why did Puck give Bottom a donkey's head? What else could have been used?*

You might extend the discussion. In Shakespeare's time, many people were superstitious, so the idea of fairies and magic terrified them. Ask students questions about superstitions:

» *Are you superstitious of things?*
» *What do you think of Bottom's shift from amateur actor to a donkey-headed character waited on by fairies?*

4. Move and speak—Speak, Pyramus. Thisby, stand forth.

> » **MATERIALS:**
> text on white board or chart paper, music (optional)
>
> » **FOCUS:**
> explore group movement and voice
>
> » **SUGGESTED TIME:**
> 15 minutes

GROUP MOVEMENT (PUPPETS ON STRINGS). In the open space of the classroom, guide students through a series of physical movements. Ask everyone to focus on the instructions you will offer. You might opt to use music for this activity. Almost like a choir director or orchestra conductor, lead students with your hands and voice to direct them:

"*Come forward very slowly and...*"

Use another hand signal:

"*Stop. Now, bend down, lower, lower, until you are lying on the ground.*"

"*Then rise, rise, and reach for the sky.
March in position, almost like soldiers.
Lean your bodies slowly one way, and now the other, arms extended.*"

After leading students through a variety of movements, you can ask one of them to replace you, and that student can guide the group. This activity mirrors Puck's magical powers as he manipulates the various workers and Athenians to and fro, around the wood, almost as if they were puppets on strings.

> I liked the music and moving. We were like floting on water. It was like dance class. —STUDENT

MIRROR GAME. An extension and more individualized activity is the mirror game. In pairs, standing a few feet apart, one student is the leader and the other is the "mirror." The leader begins by making gentle, controlled movements, which are duplicated by the other student, like a mirror. The goal is to mirror the partner perfectly, so the leader should move carefully and not try to trick his or her partner. After a minute or two, the students can switch roles. Eye contact and focus are crucial, and giggles are normal at the beginning. Once students become accustomed to this activity, someone observing could hardly recognize who is the leader.

EXPLORE VOICE. This activity introduces how voice can transform meaning and this focus is developed further in Lesson 8. Explain to students that, in the play, Quince says the line: "Speak, Pyramus. Thisby, stand forth." Ask students to work in pairs to find variations for saying Quince's line. If you wish, write the line on a white board in large letters for everyone to see. Have partners identify themselves as A and B. Ask students in group A to role play Quince, saying the line in a firm manner. Then students in group B can respond with the same line but using an opposite tone, such as a very mild, almost scared voice. Have students try the line again but reversed: B says the line in a firm manner and A responds with a mild approach. Ask students to experiment with speaking the line in different ways (excited, loud, whisper, questioning, slow, very fast, angry, happy) and responding with the opposite.

Ask students to find new partners to work on exploring Titania's line: "What angel wakes me from my flowery bed?" Again, ask students to experiment with different approaches and their opposites.

Now that I have been doing Shakespeare with primary kids for a few years, I've realized that I need to introduce text work (i.e., words or phrases, sentences, or paragraphs) more often. There are many ways to speak each line and helping them explore different options is very helpful. —TEACHER

- **MATERIALS:** dream journal
- **FOCUS:** write/draw and respond
- **SUGGESTED TIME:** 15 minutes

5. Debriefing and journal reflections

See Lesson 1 (page 65) for suggested ways of inviting students to **debrief** orally and reflect in their writing journals.

> Finding activities that develop ensemble and individual work in the classroom is important to me, as I always try to vary things. Some of my students prefer working in a large group so they are not the centre of attention. My shy students jump in more easily in the group activities. Some of my students, though, like doing activities where they are in the centre—like in the "what are you doing" game. —TEACHER

> The messiness of doing drama in the classroom should not be feared by teachers. Listening to 25 students speaking a line of Shakespeare out loud, while randomly walking around the classroom looks chaotic. This is quite different from the previous activity where soft music was playing and the entire group was harmoniously moving to the guidance of their teacher. Drama and learning is often about order and chaos, control and loss of control. It is about pushing students towards the edge, scaffolding their learning yet challenging them to explore and grow (Fels and Belliveau 2008). —RESEARCHER/OBSERVER

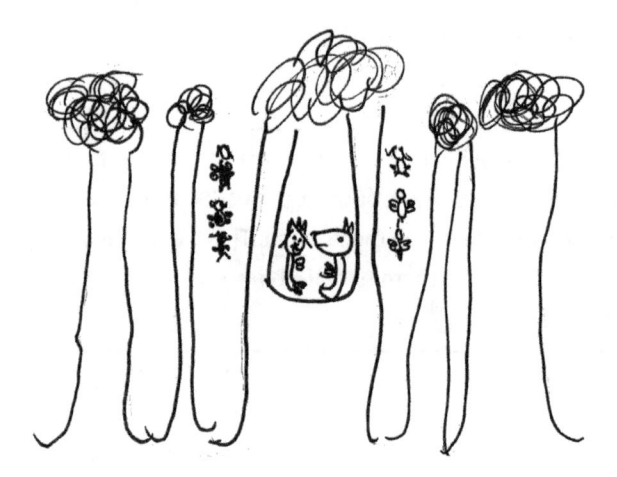

Titania falls in love with a donkey.

LESSON 6:
LOVERS' QUARREL

1. Warm-up activities

SOUNDSCAPE. In the wood there are many sounds. Lead students to walk in the space and create a **soundscape**:

> *Think about the sounds of the wind, when it hits the leaves, trees, and bushes. Think of the sounds of small animals, birds, frogs, crickets, bees, and the sounds of fairies whispering and laughing.... Using your voice and perhaps with the help of your hands, begin to improvise noises from an imagined wood."*

Once students have created a variety of sounds, ask them to stop moving, stand still as if they were trees, and continue with their sounds. While they continue with their sounds, move around the space in role as someone hesitantly walking within the imagined wood.

> *When I stop moving, you will stop your sounds.*
> *Yet, when I begin to move, your sounds begin again."*

Repeat the movements a few times, so the students get a sense of starting and stopping. The idea is that the sounds are inside the head of the person walking. Once they are familiar with the exercise, have students take turns leading the rest of the class to make or stop sounds by walking and stopping.

- » **MATERIALS:** none
- » **FOCUS:** ensemble work and sound
- » **SUGGESTED TIME:** 5–7 minutes

> My kids loved making loud forest sounds. It gave them permission to break the rules. It did take time to practise when to stop and start though! Patience is necessary. —TEACHER

If time permits, **debrief** students about the warm-up activity by asking them to briefly share their experiences.

> I made a loud owl sound. Nick made a monkey sound. It was cool walking in our woods. —STUDENT

- **MATERIALS:** story (Appendix E)
- **FOCUS:** listen and respond
- **SUGGESTED TIME:** 10 minutes

2. Introduce vocabulary

> **prank**—*noun*—a trick, joke, mischievous act
> **canker-blossom**—*noun*—a plant eaten by disease or infection
> **maiden**—*adjective*—of an unmarried girl or woman
> **counterfeit**—*noun*—a fake, imitation, or forgery
> **overcast**—*verb*—to cover with clouds or darkness

The words are taken from the story portion and defined. Prepare cue cards for the vocabulary and share the words one at a time. Use the same approach as in Lesson 1 (page 62).

3. Read the adapted story

You might begin by asking your students what occurred in the story in the previous lesson, and review with them key moments and characters so far. See Lesson 1 (page 63) for ideas and suggestions on ways to introduce the story portion to your class.

Lovers' Quarrel

Puck is delighted with the **prank** on Titania (making her fall in love with a donkey) and tells Oberon about it. Oberon then asks Puck about the love potion for the Athenian. Just then, they see Hermia and Demetrius, so discover that Puck has put the love juice on the *wrong* young man. Angrily, Oberon insists that Puck fix this mistake: Puck is to find and bring Helena while Oberon anoints Demetrius' eyes as he sleeps so that he will wake to love Helena. Within moments, Oberon and Puck do their magic, and Demetrius now rightly loves Helena.

However, all is not well yet. Lysander is still under the effect of the love juice, so remains in love with Helena. A quarrel starts between the two men as they both fight in vain for Helena. While the men quarrel, the long-time friends Helena and Hermia engage in a fight of wit.

> HERMIA: You **canker-blossom**! *You thief of love!*
> *What, have you come by night*
> *And stolen my love's heart from him?*

*HELENA: Have you no modesty, no **maiden** shame?*
*Fie, fie! You **counterfeit**, you puppet, you!*
HERMIA: Puppet? Why so? How low am I, thou painted maypole!

In Athens, both men loved Hermia, while Helena loved Demetrius. But now in the wood, through Puck and Oberon's trickeries, *both* men love Helena. Hermia is angry about losing Lysander's love. Feeling mocked, Helena is furious.

In a playful manner, Puck **overcasts** the night and leads the lovers in the various directions in the wood before making them all fall asleep. Once the young Athenians are asleep on the ground, Puck uses the love juice to make everything right. When they awake, Demetrius will love Helena, Lysander will love Hermia, and all will be well.

Here are some suggested questions for discussion:

» *In what ways might you see comedy within the mistakes?*
» *What role is Puck playing in this series of mistakes? Should he be to blame? If so, why?*
» *Why are Helena and Hermia arguing? Do you think something has been lost in their friendship? If so, what and why?*
» *If the young Athenians wake from their spell, what do you think they might remember?*

4. Retell narrative: Woods come to life

SPEAKING WOOD. In this activity, invite students to become part of the forest and speak as animals, trees, or any other object found there. For example, you might begin the action as a tree and prepare some students in advance to become birds, rabbits, or other creatures:

» **TREE:** *I've been standing in this wood for nearly 100 years and I have never seen anything like this craziness. Humans usually just come for a walk. They might tug at one of my branches. But those two girls, they were really mad. And so were the boys.*
» **BIRD:** *I've been flying around this wood for some time, and I have noticed Puck do some nasty things to people. I think he likes to trick*

» **MATERIALS:** none
» **FOCUS:** role-playing, imagination, and improvised voices
» **SUGGESTED TIME:** 10 minutes

the humans. I saw him put juice on the Athenian youths, and then laugh out loud.

» **RABBIT:** *I've been hopping around the wood and I saw this girl Helena. I feel bad for the girl because she was treated horribly by the boys. With my big ears I heard everything, and I know both boys love her!*

Workers rehearsing their play.

> I was scard to say any thing at first. Ellen said I'm a butterfly, and I think Helena is nice, the boys are being mean. I was a squrrl. I wanted to help Hermia so I put a spell on Lysander. —STUDENT

Invite more students (not briefed) to enter into the scene, becoming another part of the wood and commenting on the action from the story. As students enter, the wood comes to life to tell its story, allowing students to extend the story from additional perspectives. Once students enter the scene, they should stay in place to create the wood and its surroundings. For instance, the tree would stay frozen in place as other animals or objects share a narrative.

> I needed to prepare my students for this activity. I reminded them to use their imagination and that there is no right or wrong way of participating, as long as they stay on topic. After a few students entered the scene others were more able to see possibilities. We had crickets, snails, spiders, logs, you name it!—TEACHER

Once a number of students have entered the action you might clear the scene and start again to give those standing a break and allow new voices in. You might then extend the activity by having the animals, trees, plants, rocks, and so on engage in conversation with one another, sharing what they saw or heard someone else say. You might also include the Athenians in this activity by having two of your students play Helena and Hermia, enter the wood, and use the speech in the story portion. The speaking wood could then respond to what just happened. (See scene 2 of Role Drama 1 (pages 33–34) for a variation on this activity.)

5. Debriefing and journal reflections

See Lesson 1 (page 65) for suggested ways of inviting students to **debrief** orally and reflect in their writing journals. Students might share or write about the story the wood told in the last activity. *What were some of the voices? How were they different?*

> » **MATERIALS:** dream journal
>
> » **FOCUS:** write/draw and respond
>
> » **SUGGESTED TIME:** 15 minutes

The ensemble work in the last activity only succeeds if everyone is working and creating together (Anderson 2012). The earlier lessons help to scaffold skill levels and group dynamics so the class is now ready to do more advanced work and take greater risks with their creativity (Beare 2011). It is important to keep doing warm-up games as this ritual prepares the students to further explore their use of body and voice in the later drama activities. The act of creating the sounds of the wood in the first activity [soundscape] builds to the second one [speaking wood] where students embody and personify animals and objects, which is key to developing multi-sensory learning and awareness (Baldwin 2012). —RESEARCHER/OBSERVER

Puck tries to make things right.

ENGAGING WITH THE STORY OF *A MIDSUMMER NIGHT'S DREAM*

LESSON 7:
RELEASE OF SPELLS AND ALL IS WELL

- » **MATERIALS:** none
- » **FOCUS:** ensemble work, body movement
- » **SUGGESTED TIME:** 5 minutes

1. Warm-up activity

BODY DOMINOES. Ask students to stand and form a large circle.

"*Everyone gently tilt your heads to your right. Now gently to your left....*"

Repeat a few times, gently warming up students' necks with slow rotations and twists.

"*Now bend forward with a straight back from your waist. Bend at your waist to the left side, doing a small tilt, and now do the same to the right side. One more time....*"

Repeat a few times, gently warming up students' backs with gentle bends, twists, and pivots.

Now turn or pivot your head gently to the right and tell the student to your right to do the same, and then that student tells the next person, and the next, around the circle like dominoes.

"*Just turn your head gently.*"

Go around the circle twice.

"*Let's try the other direction, to the left.*"

Go around the circle twice in the other direction.

"*Now, from above your hips, twist your upper body to the left, and let's create a domino effect around the circle.*"

Go around the circle twice.

"*Let's try the other direction, to your right, twisting your upper body.*"

STEPPING INTO DRAMA

Go around the circle twice.

You might also decide to add a slight variation by introducing sound when students twist, such as *aah, ooh*.

If time permits, **debrief** students about the warm-up activity by asking them to briefly share their experiences.

This builds on previous activities with a slight variation. Having done previous community building activities like this one, they quickly get it's about the group and not the individual. —TEACHER

---

2. Introduce vocabulary

> » MATERIALS: cue cards, word wall
> » FOCUS: build understanding and vocabulary
> » SUGGESTED TIME: 5 minutes

slumber—*noun*—sleep, such as a nap
concord—*noun*—agreement or harmony
overrule—*verb*—to make a decision at a higher level that rejects an earlier decision
feast—*noun*—meal with plenty of food and drink
solemnity—*noun*—a feeling of formality, seriousness, such as at a wedding

The words are taken from the story portion and defined. Prepare cue cards for the vocabulary and share the words one at a time. Use the same approach as in Lesson 1 (page 62).

3. Read the adapted story

> » MATERIALS: story (Appendix E)
> » FOCUS: listen and respond
> » SUGGESTED TIME: 10 minutes

You might begin by asking your students what occurred in the story in the previous lesson, and review with them key moments and characters so far. See Lesson 1 (page 63) for ideas and suggestions on ways to introduce the story portion to your class.

Release of Spells and All Is Well

Oberon and Puck quietly approach Titania's bower to observe the donkey-loving Queen. Feeling sorry for Titania, Oberon releases the spell from her and tells Puck to remove the donkey head from Bottom. Titania and Bottom, now relieved of their spells, wonder how these things came to pass. Was it a dream? Hand in hand, Oberon and Titania leave with a sense of having resolved their differences.

Nearby, Theseus, Hippolyta, and Egeus discover the young Athenians sleeping on the dirty ground. With horns and their voices, the royal couple and Egeus wake them from their **slumber**.

*THESEUS: I pray you all, stand. How comes this gentle **concord** in the woods?*
LYSANDER: My lord, I shall reply amazedly,
Half sleep, half waking: but as yet, I swear,
I cannot truly say how I came here.

Still furious, Egeus is determined to have his daughter Hermia obey his wishes and marry Demetrius. However, Demetrius now swears his love for Helena. Theseus **overrules** the law of Athens, so that "three and three, we'll hold a **feast** in great **solemnity**." There will be a triple wedding at the palace! On their walk out of the wood and back to Athens, the young lovers try to figure out what has happened. Was it a dream?

Here are some suggested discussion questions:

» *Why do you think Titania forgave Oberon?*
» *What do you think will happen to Bottom and Puck?*
» *Theseus says, "three and three we'll hold a feast in great solemnity." What does he mean by "three and three" and why do you think Theseus and Hippolyta made this decision?*

4. Flashback to trace the young Athenians' journey—was it a dream?

- » **MATERIALS:** Young Athenians' Journey (Appendix F)
- » **FOCUS:** track the journey of characters
- » **SUGGESTED TIME:** 20 minutes

TABLEAU COLLAGE. This activity aims to track and present the four young Athenians through *Dream* prior to the wedding in the final act, which is the resolution of the story and play. Divide the class into four groups so that each group will track the actions of the young Athenians in one act. Groups can have up to six students as the acts involve the four Athenians (Helena, Hermia, Lysander, and Demetrius) and other characters. You might need to explain that each "act" is a part of a play and *Dream* is a play in five acts. Assign each group one of the first four acts and provide them with the information for their act from the Young

Athenians' Journey handout (Appendix F), either by photocopying and handing out copies or projecting it. Give the groups 3–5 minutes to review the actions in their assigned act.

Ask each group to develop two tableaux showing the progression or development of relationships between Helena, Hermia, Lysander, Demetrius, and other possible characters within their given act. Give the groups at least five minutes to develop and practise their tableaux. They may (and should) include other characters, such as Egeus, Puck, Oberon, or the fairies.

To help distinguish the four young Athenians in each act, it would be useful to provide one prop each for Helena, Hermia, Demetrius, and Lysander. For example, a coloured sash (possibly with the character's name), or a scarf, or belt. It's important that the props be easy to put on and take off, as you may opt to have Helena in group 1, for instance, pass her sash or prop to Helena in group 2, and so on, with each character handing on his or her prop for each act. The exchanging of props can be done in character and become part of the group process.

After doing a dress rehearsal and practising the sequence of exchanging props, ask students to present their tableaux in order. The group for Act 1 presents its first and second tableaux, then the group for Act 2, then Act 3, and so on. In this way, they will summarize the journey of the Athenians from the beginning of the play until the end. It's best to share the tableau sequences in a circle format so that each group can readily see the work of their peer groups.

If time permits, an extension to this activity could be for each group to create tableaux depicting future relationships amongst the four Athenians, after they are married. These extension tableaux involve predicting how the relationships will unfold.

5. Debriefing and journal reflections

See Lesson 1 (page 65) for suggested ways of inviting students to debrief orally and reflect in their writing journals. They might write about the characters they played during the last activity and predict their lives after they are married.

» **MATERIALS:** dream journal

» **FOCUS:** write/draw and respond

» **SUGGESTED TIME:** 15 minutes

The plot involving Helena, Hermia, Lysander, and Demetrius is complex. By tracing their journeys through these tableaux, students begin to understand more clearly who is who and what is going on. It also ties the beginning of the play to the end with the preparation of a marriage that was interrupted. —TEACHER

The comfort and playfulness of doing drama activities over the last few weeks naturally leads towards the text work in the upcoming lesson. The fear of trying new things has been lessened and students are ready to tackle Shakespeare's language (Belliveau 2012). They see the language as play and something to try out in different tones and voices. Shakespeare's characters are bigger than life—and bring to this the innocence and insouciance of children—and we have the perfect recipe for creative expression.
—RESEARCHER/OBSERVER

Releasing the spells.

This is when queen titania falls in love with Nick Bottom King Oberon is hiding behind the rock He told Puck to fix the problem.

Dream journal entry.

LESSON 8:
PLAY WITHIN THE PLAY ON THE WEDDING DAY

1. Warm-up activities

SHAKE DOWN. Have students find a space in the classroom to loosen up by shaking their bodies. Make sure there is enough space so they do not bump into one another, and lead them with the following instructions and countdowns.

> *Shake your:*
> | | | | |
> |---|---|---|---|
> | right hand | 5-4-3-2-1 | right hand | 4-3-2-1 |
> | left hand | 5-4-3-2-1 | left hand | 4-3-2-1 |
> | right arm | 5-4-3-2-1 | right arm | 4-3-2-1 |
> | left arm | 5-4-3-2-1 | left arm | 4-3-2-1 |
> | right foot | 5-4-3-2-1 | right foot | 4-3-2-1 |
> | left foot | 5-4-3-2-1 | left foot | 4-3-2-1 |
> | right leg | 5-4-3-2-1 | right leg | 4-3-2-1 |
> | left leg | 5-4-3-2-1 | left leg | 4-3-2-1"|

> » **MATERIALS:** none
> » **FOCUS:** body and voice control
> » **SUGGESTED TIME:** 3 minutes for each warm-up activity

Repeat each again with 3-2-1 counts, then repeat with 2-1, and finally 1. In other words, the activity gets progressively faster with smaller numbers.

You can count forwards from 1–5 as well. You can also extend it to 10 as the students get faster and more comfortable with the activity.

> This is my favourite activity. James and I always ask to do Shake Down. It's fun and wakes us up. —STUDENT

TONGUE TWISTERS. Ask students to repeat after you the following tongue twisters—and repeat each at least two or three times.

» *The lips, and the teeth, and the tip of the tongue*
» *Red fish, blue fish*
» *A big black bug bit a big black bear and made the big black bear bleed blood.*
» *Red leather, yellow leather*
» *Sweet Moon, I thank thee for thy sunny beams; thy gracious, golden, glittering gleams.*

> I usually do the tongue twisters orally, with my students repeating after me. Lately though, I started writing them out on chart paper and posting them in the class. Occasionally I would find them written in their journals with variations or additions. —TEACHER

If time permits, **debrief** students about the warm-up activities by asking them to briefly share their experiences.

2. Introduce vocabulary

> » **MATERIALS:** cue cards, word wall
>
> » **FOCUS:** build understanding and vocabulary
>
> » **SUGGESTED TIME:** 5 minutes

preferred—*verb*—wanted, chosen over others
climax—*noun*—most exciting part of the story or play, the high point of interest
star-crossed—*adjective*— unfortunate, unlucky
festivities—*noun*—celebration

The words are taken from the story portion and defined. Prepare cue cards for the vocabulary and share the words one at a time. Use the same approach as in Lesson 1 (page 62).

3. Read the adapted story

> » **MATERIALS:** story (Appendix E)
>
> » **FOCUS:** listen and respond
>
> » **SUGGESTED TIME:** 10 minutes

You might begin by asking your students what occurred in the story in the previous lesson, and review with them key moments and characters so far. See Lesson 1 (page 63) for ideas and suggestions on ways to introduce the story portion to your class.

Play Within the Play on the Wedding Day

Released from his donkey head, Bottom returns to the group of actors, who are relieved and delighted to see him. "O most happy hour!" Quince exclaims. Not only is Bottom returned, but news has arrived that their play is **preferred**! They will perform *Pyramus and Thisby* for the Duke and Duchess on their wedding night.

In front of the joyful Athenians at the palace, the workers-turned-actors nervously perform their play. A number of mishaps take place during the show as the amateur actors—led by the over-acting, over-eager Bottom—do their best to please. And please they do! But, their tragedy turns out to be more of a comedy, with Wall, Moonshine, and Lion explaining their parts to the audience rather than performing. At the **climax** of the tragedy, when the **star-crossed** lovers Pyramus and Thisby take their lives, the audience is in tears. But these are tears of laughter rather than tears of sadness. The actors are thanked, but kindly asked to leave as their efforts are now done. Theseus and Hippolyta and the four young Athenians enjoyed the **festivities** and are now newly wed. To end the story, Puck invites us all to think of this play as a dream and to put our hands together, "if we be friends," and clap in appreciation.

Here are some suggested discussion questions:

» *What do you think Bottom said to his fellow actors about his transformed experience?*
» *What do we know about the play? What experience did the actors have? What was the response from the audience?*
» *If* Dream *continued for another act, what do you think would happen?*

4. Listen to some text

SPOTLIGHT ON VOICE. Copy the two speeches below, reproduced with line numbers and letters in Appendix G.

» The speech from Bottom comes from the play's Act 5, scene 1 and is numbered lines 1–13.
» The speech from Oberon is from Act 2, scene 1 and lettered lines A–K.

» **MATERIALS:** hearing the text activity (Appendix G)
» **FOCUS:** think and question in role
» **SUGGESTED TIME:** 20 minutes

In total, there are 24 lines in the speeches. If there are more than 24 students in your class, you might wish to have two students with the same line of text or add a third speech. If you have fewer than 24 students, you can simply delete some lines, or have some children speak more than one line each.

Cut the lines into strips and provide each student with one strip of paper. Direct students to individually practise saying their particular line of text from the strip of paper in different ways as they walk in the classroom space.

> "*You can say it in a very happy way, an angry way, softly, loudly, as if it were a question, as if you were speaking to a cat or dog, as if you were a TV broadcaster...*"

After giving students some time to experiment with their line of text (about two minutes), ask them to form two lines.

> *You each have a number or a letter on your strip of paper. Numbers 1–13 stand on the right side, beginning with 1 at the front and 13 at the back. Now, on the other side of the room, letters A–K line up beginning with A."*

Once students are lined up in their two rows, direct them to turn so that the two rows are back to back, not facing one another. This makes it more about their voices, as no one is looking at one another directly.

> *Now, when I count down to 1, I want you all to read your lines of text together using whatever voice seems appropriate."*

And count down 3-2-1. It should be chaotic and loud with everyone reading at once!

> *Repeat your lines one more time all together, and this time speak as if you were talking with your outside, loud voice."*

Pause. Now ask for the lines of Bottom's speech in sequence:

> *This time, one at a time, numbers 1–13, speak your lines one after the other in an outside voice. Number 1 begin with Sweet Moon..."*

If needed, direct students to gently nudge, or to turn to, the next student when they have completed their line, signalling it is that student's turn.

I found it helpful to have the Bottom and Oberon groups sit in separate circles to discuss the speeches. This allowed them the opportunity to consider the meaning and context, as well as what voice to use for their collective lines. —TEACHER

Now ask for the lines of Oberon's speech in sequence:

> *Now, students with letters A–K, speak your lines one after the other in an outside voice. Letter A, begin with "I pray thee..."*

STEPPING INTO DRAMA

Again, encourage students to help the person next to them, by indicating that they're done (for example, by nudging or turning to that person at the end of their line).

Ask them to repeat the speeches a few times, and guide them to experiment with different voices. For example, you might have students share their lines as if they were telling a deep secret or reporting on a news broadcast.

If time permits, you might suggest that they add some small movements. The two groups could then face each other and share their collective speeches one after the other.

BOTTOM:
1. *Sweet Moon, I thank thee for thy sunny beams;*
2. *Thy gracious, golden, glittering gleams.*
3. *But stay, O spite! What dreadful dole is here!*
4. *Eyes, do you see? How can it be?*
5. *Thy mantle good, What, stain'd with blood!*
6. *Lion vile hath here deflower'd my dear:*
7. *Which is—no, no—which was the fairest dame*
8. *That lived, that loved, that liked, that look'd.*
9. *Come, tears, confound; Out, sword, and wound*
10. *Thus die I, thus, thus, thus.*
11. *Now am I dead, Now am I fled;*
12. *Tongue, lose thy light; Moon take thy flight:*
13. *Now die, die, die, die, die.*

OBERON:
A. *I pray thee, give it me.*
B. *I know a bank where the wild thyme blows,*
C. *Where ox lips and the nodding violet grows,*
D. *There sleeps Titania. There I'll streak her eyes,*
E. *And make her full of hateful fantasies.*
F. *Take thou some of it, gentle Puck,*
G. *A sweet Athenian lady is in love*
H. *With a disdainful youth: anoint his eyes;*
I. *But do it when the next thing he espies*
J. *May be the lady: thou shalt know the man*
K. *By the Athenian garments he hath on.*

- **MATERIALS:** dream journal
- **FOCUS:** write/draw and respond
- **SUGGESTED TIME:** 15 minutes

5. Debriefing and journal reflections

See Lesson 1 (page 65) for suggestions on ways of inviting students to **debrief** orally and reflect in their writing journals.

At this point they are ready for the script. They know the story and the characters, and they are desperate to find out what part they will play. By giving them various pieces of the play,...they now have a taste of the characters and they are more ready to give their opinion on which part they'd like to be. —TEACHER

My favourite moment was when my daughter started reading scenes of the play to me. I spent years in high school and college with Shakespeare's work, and feel that it is familiar because I have worked so hard to learn it. But I remember the feeling of dealing with Shakespeare for the first time in grade 10— just this intense trepidation because it was so strange and so hard—and to see my daughter pick up the text and start reading it to me, with the confidence that she could do it because she knew the play, in grade two! It's so cool that they feel such familiarity with such a difficult author; really, as readers, it makes them unstoppable. —PARENT

Workers perform on the wedding day.

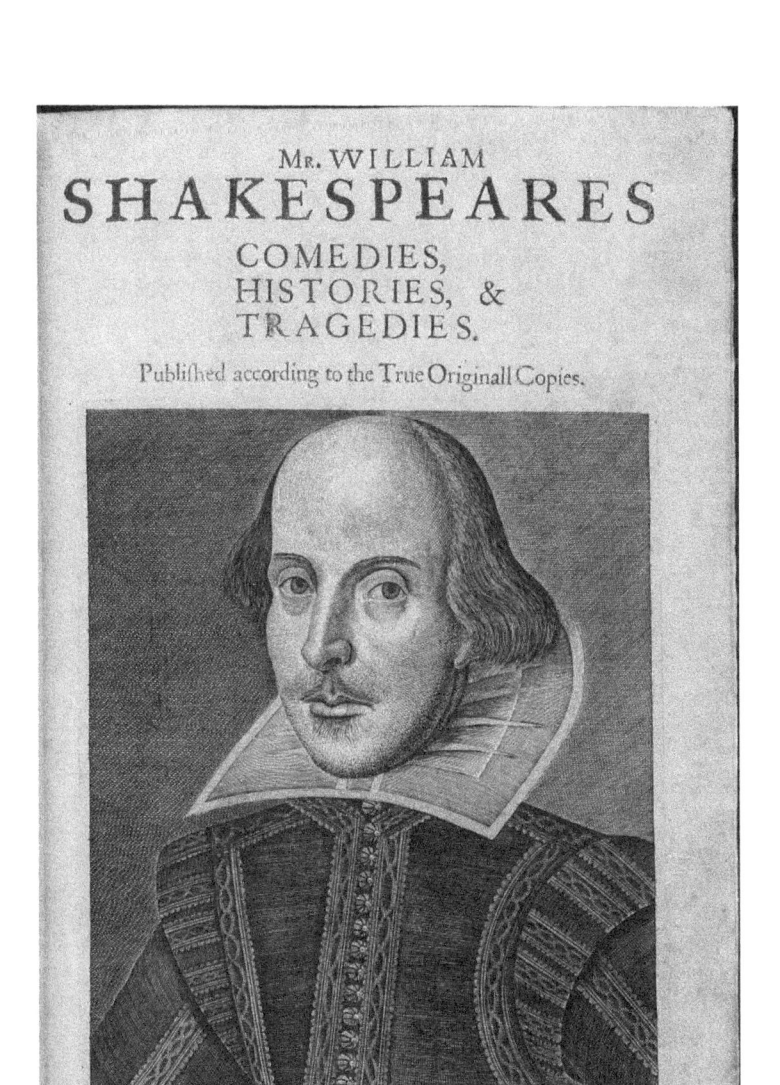

This portrait of William Shakespeare, engraved by Martin Droeshout, appeared on the title page of the first published collection of Shakespeare's plays in 1623.

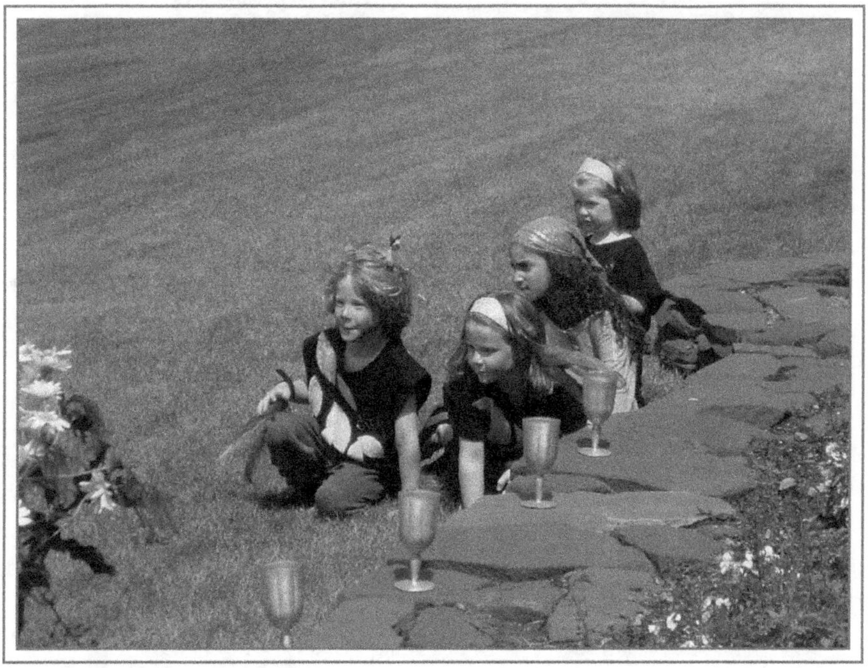

PART IV

FROM PAGE TO STAGE: SHARING THE PLAY ADAPTATION

THIS SECTION PROVIDES INSIGHTS, STRATEGIES, AND SUPPORT FOR preparing, rehearsing, and producing a class presentation of *Dream* using the play adaptation, which is found in Part V. Specifically, this part includes the following:

- a possible production schedule
- consideration of production elements, including tips and ideas
- a suggested schedule for rehearsals
- strategies to help you and your students rehearse the play

The demands of the classroom often make it difficult to have large blocks of time to rehearse a play. As a result, the suggestions here offer flexibility and opportunities where small groups of students can rehearse scenes while others might work on other aspects of the curriculum.

Less Is More

A common theatre motto is that "less is more"; this pertains to costumes, sets, props, music, visuals, blocking, and all other aspects of your production. Keeping Shakespeare's language and character development at the centre of the work helps tell the story and keeps the focus on the students and their work. When there are too many distractions and things to see and to remember (for example, moving Titania's bed or bringing in small trees for the wood), the play becomes more about these production elements than the acting and storytelling of the students. The same is true for costumes and hand props; they should be limited so the play does not become about putting on a hat or belt correctly. While costumes and props can help establish ambience, they can also detract from the pedagogical focus of the work. Most set pieces and props can be imagined by the audience, so *use only what is necessary*. Shakespeare's text often provides clear descriptions of locations within the dialogue, and his plays were written with minimal sets in mind because they were originally performed on mostly bare stages. Blocking should also be controlled, so that characters are moving with purpose rather than out of nervousness and uncertainty. For more about these and other staging considerations, see the coming pages.

> I have to be honest: it's sometimes totally overwhelming and I often ask myself, why am I doing this? I must be going nuts! The role dramas and drama activities while reading the story are all fine and manageable. But when I get to the production, I begin to get nervous, even after doing this for 6–7 years. I think: "How can these 6 to 8-year-olds memorize these lines? What are we going to use for costumes, backdrop, props?" It feels like this huge mountain. Then I breathe deeply and I think, "OK, one step at a time." I ask the students what theme they would like for our play. From their suggestions, we then get ideas for the costumes. Parents then always offer to help. Our chosen theme often guides the music, where one or two students take leadership with the keyboard, recorder, or other instruments. *I gradually begin to breathe normally again!* A few students come in with their lines memorized, which then motivates others. Their characters begin to develop, and our voice work finally seems to help as the students enunciate more clearly and they are louder. Step by step, the production and rehearsals take us a little closer to *telling the story*. Each year is different and the route to the production changes with the given group of students. Trusting the process and having a schedule keeps us moving forward, and we go as far as we can in the time we have together. I can't deny that it is always the most challenging and nerve-wracking part of my year, but I wouldn't want it any other way. The rewards are immeasurable for me and for them. It's the highlight of the year. —TEACHER

PRODUCTION CONSIDERATIONS

Thus far, the emphasis in this book has been on the process of introducing children to Shakespeare. In building towards the production of a 30-minute adaptation of *Dream*, the focus continues to be on the learning along the way. In other words, the focus should not be a final product consisting of a polished performance but rather the learning throughout that process and a sharing of the students' learning and creativity with others. Just as a marathon is the victory lap of months of training, celebrating hundreds of kilometres run in preparation for the race, the same is true with your elementary class' production of Shakespeare.

The schedule below offers suggestions for considering production elements for your class sharing of the play. It elaborates on the schedules introduced in Part I. It runs *concurrently* with the rehearsal schedule found later in this part, on page 115. In other words, the anticipated time on production and rehearsal combined is a total of six weeks, not twelve.

Sample Production Schedule: Six Weeks

WEEK	MONDAY	TUESDAY	WEDNESDAY	THURSDAY	FRIDAY
1		**Cast** students in roles	Hand out copies of script		
2		Decide on **space and setting** for play	Determine dates for production		
3		Decide theme of play	Create **props, costumes**, and set lists		
4		Brainstorm music, **sound**, image, and **lighting** ideas	Bring in props for rehearsal		
5	Bring in costumes and **set pieces**	Create invitation list	Create and distribute **program** and poster	Finalize music, sound, image, and lighting	
6	Dress rehearsal (no audience)	Dress rehearsal (invite another class)	Production (invite other classes)	Production (invite friends and family)	

NOTE: The production considerations that appear on the calendar in boldface are discussed in detail below.

Casting

Casting is typically done once the students are familiar with the story and they have engaged with the characters and the language. At this point they are more ready to take the script and understand where their character fits into the play as a whole.

Asking students which role they would like to play is a helpful exercise. For instance, you can ask each student to list on a piece of paper three roles they would like to play. However, it should be made clear to students that asking to play a particular role does not assure being cast in that role. Challenging your students with certain parts is a great way for them to aim higher in their learning, but you must also be careful not to overwhelm students.

The casting of roles should be done in a manner that offers opportunities for as many students as possible. Therefore, double-casting and even triple-casting a role might be an option. It is not unusual to have productions with four Pucks, possibly playing the role at the same time, speaking in chorus, and sometimes with solo voices. In certain cases, having two entirely separate casts may work better for your class, particularly in the upper elementary grades, where you have a number of students able to undertake large roles. With the younger grades, it is especially useful to have two or more students play each larger role so that one student plays a major character for the first half, and another student undertakes the role for the second half. To help audiences recognize the switch, the different actors might use similar costumes for the one character. You could also create a moment in which one actor "hands off" the character to the other actor. For example, the two actors playing Puck could meet at centre stage wearing similar costumes, face each other, perform a 360-degree turn together, and the second actor continues while the first leaves the stage, thus signalling to the audience a change in cast.

Depending on your class, you might decide to involve some students in group scenes of people or to represent objects in the scenes. These opportunities might develop during rehearsal.

Teacher Taking on a Role

The default position of many teachers is to be the director, a role not unlike the daily role of a teacher guiding a class through various activities. You will inevitably be part of the directing team for a class production. However, if you are also able to be one of the actors, this allows you to "play" alongside the students within the world of Shakespeare. In *Dream*, you might play a part such as Quince, Snug, or Snout. As you memorize lines, create a costume, and become nervous about performing, you become part of the company of actors with your students, instead of always being in charge and in control. By taking a role within the play, you release some of the power and authority of the teacher. Students can become quite excited by having their teacher in the play, and it can increase their commitment and level of playing. In upper elementary classes, you might assign particular students to direct some scenes, giving them leadership opportunities.

> I once cast a very capable grade 2 student as Oberon from my multi-age grade 1–3 classroom. He seemed to be up for the challenge; however, the next year, he asked to play a much smaller part. He did not want to have the responsibility of such a large role again. —TEACHER

> One of my more timid grade 5 girls wanted to play Titania, and I was initially hesitant. I wasn't sure she could hold the part. This timid child rose a

few inches taller when she was cast in the role. She then proceeded to play Titania with authority and dignity, lifting her confidence and showing her talent and commitment. —TEACHER

Space and Setting

Each school and classroom is unique and offers different possibilities and challenges in terms of space for the production. In a number of older schools, the gym has a stage area where assemblies, concerts, graduation, and other special events take place. The acoustics of these stage areas often make it challenging for young voices to be heard. Also, creative use of space—such as having the audience seated in different places—is often not possible. Furthermore, time to rehearse and set up in these spaces may be limited as they are often used for numerous school activities.

A preferable option might be a multi-purpose room with lots of open space, especially if it can be made available to your class for an extended period of time. Another option is to transform your classroom into a stage setting and have the production there.

Two fairies ready to serve their Queen.

Presenting your work in your classroom may be the optimal option, particularly for the younger children, for these reasons:

» The production is a showcase of the learning that took place within the classroom.
» A number of the activities within the role dramas and the reading of the story involve creating artifacts, such as masks, flowers, and leaves. All these pieces can be displayed on the walls, helping to transform the classroom into the world of the play.
» Younger students may be more comfortable in their own classroom and may feel less overwhelmed when it is performance time.
» The acoustics and sight lines are easier to manage in a classroom.
» You will have more flexibility with times for rehearsing and other class work; as well, you will be able to leave props, costumes, and instruments in the space between rehearsals.

However, limitations of space within a classroom can be an issue. This means the audience must remain small and the space must be managed carefully, which might result in more performances for your students!

The school custodial staff can be of great assistance during this time, as they might help you with removing and storing some of the desks or tables to give more space. As well, custodial staff should be consulted about how to safely black out class windows if you want darkness for the play, and about increased needs for electricity for lights or sound.

Lighting and Sound

A very effective and easy way to create appropriate ambience is with lighting—ranging from what is already available in your classroom to rented professional lighting equipment. Within your own classroom, you might be able to turn certain lights on and off, remove particular bulbs to focus the light in one or two particular areas, or direct others. Again, the school custodian can help with the removal of light bulbs. Desk lamps or headlamps can also be used. Let your imagination wander, but always remember to keep safety first. Renting lighting equipment from a local theatre is not as difficult as it may seem. New lighting boards are easy to use and to work with. In the upper elementary grades, you will often find very capable students who would enjoy undertaking this responsibility. Some schools and school boards own theatre lighting equipment. If you are interested in exploring this option, inquire early as such equipment is often in demand.

Sound effects and/or music provide a valuable addition to any production, so consider adding these when possible. Sound can come from pre-recorded devices or live musicians, whether singers or instrumentalists. When possible, live music is always more engaging than recordings, and it offers a chance to showcase the musicians within your class. For example, students might play (or know others who play) recorders, flutes, acoustic guitars, other string instruments, and drums. If using live music is not possible, pre-recorded sound effects and music are options. Computers or hand-held electronic devices are possible sources, and with proper speakers, the sound quality is very good within a classroom space. Software can help you, your students, a parent, or a friend mix songs, other music, and sound effects. Contemporary pop songs often have themes that relate to the story of *Dream*, and choosing such songs with your students helps bridge the world of Shakespeare with contemporary culture. If you do use pre-recorded music, however, check copyright restrictions.

Costumes and Props

Costumes do not need to be elaborate but they should be included in your production to some extent. Many times, the simple act of donning a vest and hat can help a student find his or her character; the costume allows the student to move from the everyday world and transform into someone else. Creating themes for the costumes helps establish the worlds within *Dream*—for example:

> The characters of the Duke's court and the young Athenian lovers might have purple for their theme colour, with male characters wearing vests and black pants, and female characters wearing purple skirts and scarves with white tops.
> The workers could be clothed in dark brown, tattered tops and dark pants.
> The characters of the fairy world might wear bright yellow, pink, and orange tops that are loose-fitting and dark tights for leggings. Makeup with sparkles can be added to the fairies to help create their magical appearance.

Like costumes, props are an important feature to help your class commit to the world(s) of the play but the props do not need to be elaborate. For example, Puck could carry a small sack to hold the magic herbs or a plastic flower to help cast the spells. For the character of Bottom, simply putting on a hat with ears can mark the transformation and give other performers a cue to react to.

Often a budget is not necessary for costumes and props because students might be able to bring what is needed from home. Local theatre companies or high schools with a theatre program may also be able to assist by loaning costumes and props. Thrift stores are valuable resources for items that cannot be found elsewhere. Typically there are a few parents who can assist to sew, mend, or alter costumes to make them fit the young learners.

Oberon in costume.

Set

Adding a few key set pieces in the playing area helps establish the world(s) of the play and the ambience. Creating a backdrop is a way to involve the entire class to visually represent the setting. You might do this by having students paint the backdrop or they might choose images to display using a projector. Small wooden risers or benches can be used to vary the heights on the stage and invite the actors to use different levels. Plants and flowers brought in by students can be used to create the feeling of the wood in *Dream*. As well, artifacts created during the process might be included in the set, such as the reflective leaves or flowers and the characters' masks.

Finally, while you are creating the set, consider the relationship of set, stage, and audience. For example, decide how best to seat the audience for viewing during the performance. Will a half-circle format work best, for instance?

Program

Creating a play program helps to establish the sense of an event for your students' production. As well, programs orient the audience to the cast and who does/did what, so will increase the audience's enjoyment and appreciation. Programs can be as simple or complicated as you wish, and they can often be created and produced by the students themselves. The key elements are, of course, the title of the play and the cast list. Students may also wish to add actor biographies and photos, a plot summary, and a note about the playwright to replicate professional theatre programs. Although recent word-processing and desktop publish software make creating programs easier and simpler than in the past, you might want to keep it simple (and less costly) by printing copies of your program in black and white. Also, begin early with this process as the layout and printing often take longer than anticipated.

You may wish to create a newspaper that will serve as the program and showcase to the community some of the students' writing and drawing during the process. You could combine:

» the title of the play, cast list, and so on
» selections from student journals
» newly created newspaper content, such as
  - brief articles written in pairs—for example, with images and headlines such as "Woman falls for donkey," "Athenian youth escape their home"
  - advertisements—for example, for Puck's Magic Potion on Sale
  - other common newspaper items—for example, weather forecasts, sports columns, entertainment gossip that relate to *Dream* in some capacity

Seeking Extra Help

Putting on a production, even in your classroom, is a significant undertaking. Seeking extra help is almost inevitable. Finding parents and other volunteers to help can come as a mixed blessing, and it is worth planning well in advance what specifically you need help with. Sending out e-mail notes to parents asking for specific items needed for the play can save you time and money because many parents may have extra fabric or paint at home. A parent might be happy to sew several vests if given the material. However, being specific with what you need is important. Asking for help with costumes generally, for instance, can create more work than anticipated for both you and volunteers. For example, one parent might start developing one theme, while another parent brings something entirely different and incompatible. In the end, you want to honour the offerings of all volunteers, but you need help to support and complement what you have explored with your students and in the class. Therefore, clear, specific communication is key.

In addition to parents, other teachers in the school, administrative staff, librarians, and other members of the school and local communities might wish to help. Recently retired teachers and university students wishing to be teachers might be looking for opportunities to volunteer. Many of these adults might be able to assist with one small task, such as developing the program, playing music, or rehearsing one on one with a student who needs special attention.

Starveling as Moonshine with lantern.

Make the Performance an Event

The performance is the culmination of the work you and your students have done over several months, so it is important to celebrate and share the class' accomplishments with others. While the performance is only one of many parts of the process, it is perhaps the only public event you will do with the Shakespeare text. In addition to the program or newspaper suggested earlier, you might consider:

» making invitations for the parents and school officials
» creating posters to hang up around the school and outside your door to announce the event
» asking parents to volunteer to bring food for a small cast party after the play

All these pieces add to making the production an event and celebration for the students.

REHEARSAL CONSIDERATIONS

It is critical to develop a rehearsal schedule to ensure you have dedicated blocks of time for rehearsing the play. The sample schedule following provides suggestions for a six-week rehearsal process. As noted earlier, this schedule is a complement to the production schedule on page 108 and occurs concurrently.

Scheduling 20 to 30 hours of rehearsal for a 30-minute play is usually sufficient for a class production. Asking students to work on memorizing lines at home can be part of the homework as can the journal-writing activities that support character building. The rehearsal strategies following offer techniques and suggestions to consider integrating during the six-week period. The various suggestions help students develop particular parts of the performance, as well as a spirit of team building through the process.

Sample Rehearsal Schedule: Six Weeks

WEEK	MONDAY	TUESDAY	WEDNESDAY	THURSDAY	FRIDAY
1		Read script (1 hr)	Read script (1 hr) Journal on character (30 min.)	Read script (1 hr) Journal on character (30 min.)	
2		Small groups, scene work Acts 1, 2 (1.5 hr)	Small groups, scene work Acts 3, 4 (1.5 hr)	Small groups, scene work Act 5 (1.5 hr)	
3		Character work with text (1.5 hr)	Work through entire play with a focus on voice (1.5 hr)	Feeding in lines Focus on body using text (1.5 hr)	
4		Feeding in lines Focus on body and voice (2 hrs)	Work through entire play with a focus on character (2 hrs)	Work through 1st half of play with lines memorized (2 hrs)	
5	Work through 2nd half of play with lines memorized (2 hrs)	Work through entire play with lines memorized (2 hrs)	Rehearse 1st half of play (2 hrs)	Rehearse 2nd half of play (2 hrs)	Work on entrances and exits, full play (2 hrs)
6	Dress rehearsal(s) (no audience) (3 hrs)	Dress rehearsal (invite another class) (2 hrs)	Production (invite other classes) (2 hrs)	Production (invite friends and family) (2 hrs)	

Warm-up Activities

In Part III, a number of warm-up activities were provided to help your students enter into the drama. During rehearsals, it is equally important to warm up your class prior to working with the script. Warm-up activities that are ensemble based help energize students, establish a collaborative working environment, and develop a creative, playful space. Repeating particular warm-ups during rehearsals creates a safe space and prepares students to focus. Some warm-ups to consider to maintain group focus include these found in Appendix A:

» Yes
» Pass the Energy
» Character Walks

Other options are Shake Down and some Tongue Twisters (see Part III, Lesson 8, page 97). Always begin warm-ups in a large circle to allow everyone to see each other, reinforcing that rehearsals are a team effort. For warm-ups, only 5–10 minutes is necessary, but it is time well spent to build cohesion and warm up both the body and voice.

Focus on Voice

Vocal exercises at the beginning of rehearsals both warm up student voices and create an ensemble environment. You could follow this sequence:

» gentle breathing activities
» speaking vowels, long and short
» doing tongue twisters

Within these activities, moving from whispering to speaking out loud helps with providing range in speaking. As well, doing tongue twisters slowly and then gradually faster helps with articulation and character development.

During rehearsals, the focus of the vocal exercises can sometimes be on finding the character voice for the role students are playing. Does the character speak in a high pitch, quickly, loudly, or nasally? Testing out a variety of nuances for their character voice helps students to make the role their own. Puck, for instance, is a very excitable character so Puck might speak quickly while moving from place to place on stage. Bottom might speak with an air of grandeur as he performs his interpretation of Pyramus. Focusing on voice is a key part of character building and finding the playfulness of doing theatre.

Focus on Body

Allotting time during rehearsals to help students find their character's posture and walk is also important. Attention to the body begins during the warm-up with movement activities that help focus on different parts of the body. Exploring character walks includes varying the speed or leading from different parts of the body—such as the head, chest, or stomach.

» *Does your character walk on her toes or heels?*
» *Is her walk jumpy, heavy, slow, or nimble?*
» *At different times in the play, does your character change his walk based on mood, location, or another circumstance?*

Focusing on a particular character's walk and body posture can help students who are self-conscious or fidgety, guiding them away from their own idiosyncratic movements that are sometimes distracting.

The development of body and voice awareness is a life-long process. As a result, certain students will be able to move more quickly than others in finding voice and body interpretations for their character.

Character Journal

Creating a character journal can be very helpful in defining and playing a role. Appendix H provides some questions to get students started. Add to and revise as needed. For example, upper elementary students may create a biography for their character by answering questions such as the following:

Puck casting sleeping spells

- » *Where did Hermia go to school?*
- » *Who are her friends?*
- » *Does she have particular hobbies?*
- » *Before the action of the play, what was her friendship like with Helena?*
- » *Before the action of the play, what did they do in their free time?*

Creating a character biography and journal allows students to have a more complete and complex understanding of their character's motives in the play. Students indirectly bring the fictional back-story they create into their interpretation, which helps their character live beyond what the playwright has written.

Another strategy with the character journal is to have students paraphrase all of their lines in their own modern, daily language. For instance, Egeus' line, "Full of vexation come I, against my daughter Hermia," might be written as, "I'm really angry with my daughter, and I want to talk with you about it, Theseus." This paraphrasing helps students to better understand what they are saying.

Memorization

Memorizing lines is something a number of students do quite well. The classroom is an environment where they are frequently asked to memorize (e.g., alphabet letters, sounds, numbers, verbs) and students are accustomed to it, therefore the memorization of a script is less daunting than most adults think. Providing strategies to help students memorize their lines is helpful though. Some of this may be done at home as part of a homework routine. For instance, students could read their lines out loud five times each evening, or have a family member read the other characters' lines in the scene.

In the early part of the rehearsal process, it is important to work on small sections at a time and go over them two or three times to allow the repetition to reinforce the learning. You can have different groups work on different scenes, repeating their lines and working on their character voices. This can be done without all the actors for a particular scene present.

Moving around the space can be helpful during memorization of longer speeches. For example, during the speech by Oberon (below, on the left), an actor might break down each line physically by going to certain locations and with certain movements (below, on the right).

Well, go thy way:	• walking forward, as if pushing Titania away
Thou shalt not from this grove	• moving right, kneeling to pick up imaginary dirt from the ground
Till I torment thee for this injury.	• squishing dirt with hands; then, simultaneously, throwing it down and standing
My gentle Puck, fetch me that flower;	• change of mood, an idea—moving left towards an imaginary Puck
The herb I shew'd thee once:	• moving towards the centre, in a dream-like state
The juice of it on sleeping eye-lids laid	• going around in a circle, rhythmically
Will make man or woman madly dote	• lightly moving towards the right
Upon the next live creature that it sees.	• moving quickly towards the centre to kneel

Note that these suggested movements are not meant to be staging ideas; instead they are ways to help a student memorize lines by moving around the space. The body has its own memory and can stimulate the learning of lines. Therefore, for example, when the young actor kneels and picks up dirt, the movement might help to trigger the line *"thou shalt not from this grove."*

Creating a voice recording of lines with an electronic device and then listening to them frequently can also help with memorization through the repetition of hearing.

Feeding in Lines/Prompting

Feeding in lines is a strategy for rehearsal that can help students memorize their lines. It allows actors to concentrate on body movement and characterization, because they do not have their script in their hands. As well, feeding in lines creates opportunities to have more students involved in the rehearsal process than would otherwise be the case. Feeding in lines/prompting is as if the actors have shadows behind them, feeding them the text.

At first, students usually need to read from their scripts. However, when the actors begin to get off-book (that is, no longer needing their scripts), the role of feeder/prompter is to stand behind the actors as they rehearse a scene and give the lines to an actor, when needed and without any character voice. When an actor forgets a line, he or she calls "line" and the feeder provides the line for the actor. The feeder may also provide a line if there is a substantial pause. The actors should stay in role, looking at each other in character as they listen for, and then repeat, their lines. This strategy takes some practice.

If your production has more than one student playing a particular role—for example, Titania—then the Titania not acting in the scene could feed lines to the Titania who is. This gives both Titanias an opportunity to explore fully the lines and character.

Group Scenes

Adding group scenes when possible is a helpful strategy for productions with young students. Most plays allow for scenes in which a number of characters other than those speaking are present. In *Dream*, the very first scene could be populated with servants and attendants listening to Theseus and Hippolyta sharing the good news of the upcoming wedding. A simple costume, such as a long white T-shirt with a sash or belt, could help distinguish the servants and attendants from the members of the court. Students can then quickly shift into another costume for their other roles when needed. As well, *Dream* can have many fairies who might sing and dance, or move to music at various moments. During the forest scenes, for instance, fairies can be wandering through the wood, helping the transitions of scenes by filling the stage.

Also having students play inanimate objects can be fun, help build the ensemble, and foster a group dynamic. Students can be trees in the wood by having their backs turned to the audience and their arms held up as branches, as long as they are not asked to stand for too long! Another method of creating a group scene is to use **choric voices**. For example, Puck's final speech may be presented in a chorus with students taking turns reading each line or by having the entire cast say the speech.

Staging Considerations

The process of establishing where and how actors move around the stage is referred to as blocking. For the purpose of your school-based production, the focus of the blocking should be on exploration, allowing students to find the spaces on stage that seem to work best for their characters and scenes. Using a rigidly planned blocking scheme with younger students can limit their creativity. However, if you are using lighting, there are moments when carefully planned blocking might be necessary.

Many younger actors have two tendencies: use only centre stage and stand to deliver their lines. As you and your students explore blocking, it is important to remind them to vary where the action takes place on stage and what positions they take. Make sure that some scenes take place on stage right, others on stage left, and some near the back or front. In some cases, it is helpful to have all the workers/amateur actors' scenes in one area and Titania's scenes in another, as this allows for smoother transitions and helps the young actors find their space on stage. Balancing the stage is key. If one thinks of staging as a teeter-totter, the scenes should go from one side to the other, never overloading one side for too long.

When exploring blocking, you and your students should also consider varying the levels used—for example, by standing, sitting, kneeling, or standing on risers. Actors can help off-set what others are doing on stage—for example, some kneeling or sitting while others stand. If you have access to risers, they will help to establish different levels on the stage and give the impression of different locations.

Entrances, Exits, and Transitions

In most plays, characters enter and exit several times, and this becomes an important aspect to rehearse. However, productions rarely take the time in rehearsals for this. A few rehearsals dedicated to working on the entrances and exits of characters are well worth the time. This can be part of planning for blocking and transitions between scenes.

You should strive for fluidity in entrances and exits, and how the actors and action move ahead generally—for example:

- » Anticipating the end of a scene by having actors for the next scene ready to enter helps the play flow.
- » Including music, lighting, or projections from a digital projector can help make the transitions seamless.
- » Curtains or blackouts between scenes are becoming less common in contemporary theatre because they break up the action of the play. Instead, aim to make transitions between scenes an integral part of the production.
- » You might consider having your actors sit on benches on the side of the stage when they are not in a scene. This can help the play flow smoothly and prevent actors from missing their cues because they are backstage. Also, having the entire cast on stage reduces backstage chatter.

Whatever you decide for entrances and exits, actors and transitions, you might find it useful to organize the decisions on charts and/or ask someone to take on the role of stage manager.

» A chart on each side of the stage could list the character name(s) and the act, scene, and line where the character(s) enter. The chart following is an example.
» A stage manager (possibly a parent or—better yet—one of your more organized students) could help get the actors ready to enter the stage and remind them where and when they will enter and exit.

Sample Entrance/Exit Sheet
SHOW: *A Midsummer Night's Dream*
DATES: June 10–12
ENTRANCE: Stage Right

ACT/SCENE	PAGE.LINE	CHARACTER	ENTRANCE LINE	NOTES
1/1	1.1	Theseus, Hippolyta	Top of play after music dims down	Wear crowns
1/1	1.5	Egeus	Hippolyta: "Four nights will quickly dream away the time"	Egeus has a cloak on.

Positive Feedback

Most elementary teachers do not come to teaching with a theatre background, let alone training as a director. However, most teachers possess their own developed understanding of what works on stage and what does not. Trust your instincts. Building on what is working has typically been most successful and most encouraging for the students. When directing students, use language such as the following: *When you used that strong voice at the beginning of the scene, I truly sensed that you were King Oberon! Keep that voice throughout!*

Recognize moments where your students are doing effective things because it affirms their efforts and builds their confidence. The three most frequent suggestions that you will likely have to give your students are:

1. *Speak louder*
2. *Speak slower*
3. *Face forward*

Find ways to offer these reminders in a positive manner. For example, you might make small signs with smiley faces or other fun images that say *slower* or *louder*. Creating a supportive environment rather than a critical, negative space will pay off in the end. Remember that the production is part of the students' learning journey and all the work you do is to support the curriculum. You are not training actors, but rather fostering creativity, community, curiosity, and life-long learning.

Debriefing Circles and Post-Production Letters

If at all possible, after each rehearsal, dress rehearsal, and performance, **debrief** the cast about the event in a circle. This creates a space to discuss what worked and what still needs development. It is best to continue with building on the positive. You may suggest the idea of two stars and a wish by asking individuals to tell you:

» two stars—two things that worked
» a wish—a goal they have for their *own* work, for how they might keep improving

Remind students that feedback about the work of others should remain positive.

The debriefing circle allows the cast to reflect on the performance of the class and unite. It also allows you to get the pulse of the group. The following are some of many sample comments from students during debriefing.

I was really nervous.

I was scared I'd forget my lines.

I didn't forget any lines.

I'm glad my mom was there.

There were lots of cameras.

I felt good.

If you're nervous it means you care.

We had lots of emotion in the play.

We were very quiet backstage.

It turned out really well.

It was fun. I liked saying my lines.

I was proud of myself.

I was happy to see all the parents.

I liked the part when Pyramus does his funny death.

My dad was there.

I really projected my voice.

I was able to slow down my lines.

It ended up really well.

I liked the part when Oberon and Titania were having their fight. They were really good.

After the production, you could also invite students to each write a letter to a friend or family member who was not able to attend. This writing assignment is an opportunity to share insights about their experiences of being a part of the play. The following is a sample student letter.

> Dear Enrica,
>
> I wish you could have seen the play! When we first started *A Midsummer Night's Dream*, I wasn't sure if I could memorize my lines because I had never been in a play before. When I found out that I was playing the character Titania, I was really surprised because I never thought that I would get to be Titania. At first I was worried about messing up the role, so I started memorizing my lines. When we began to practise some scenes, I found out that the play is really fun.
>
> Later on, we started to make the set. Before I knew it, we were doing our first performance for another class. I got a little nervous when I saw everyone staring at the stage but what I did was only look at the person I was talking to and focus on the conversation. I was mostly on stage with Oberon and Bottom. I am in a fight with Oberon over a human child but in the end everything is okay. I also fall in love with a donkey!
>
> When we did our final play for the parents, it was great. I didn't forget a single line! I was really happy that I didn't get prompted. The whole experience was great. I am also happy that I didn't get a small part. Playing Titania was cool. My teacher found me a dress for my character and, a week before, I made a flower crown with my mom. Doing a play was awesome! I hope I'll get to do another one next year.
>
> Your friend,

After the final performance, I'm always reminded of the journey and learning that took place for my students. I look at them and I am amazed at how far they have come. ... I realize that I'm perhaps the only one who has fully witnessed this incredible learning journey they took. The parents, cameras in hand, see their child in costume, reciting their lines, taking ownership of their part on stage. They know it took some rehearsing and memorizing, but they didn't see: the emotional side; taking on a role they might not have asked for; the fear that they may not be able to learn their part; the fear of forgetting a line or sequence of lines; the competition of memorizing their lines; the challenge of bringing the lines to life. And equally as important: laughing at themselves; enjoying the work of their peers; feeling that they're part of something bigger than they are. —TEACHER

She [a student in the class] has become fascinated with all things Shakespearean...and really wanted to see pictures of the costumes and historical paintings of the play. We spent many an hour searching the internet.... She has recently been looking into other plays with thoughts about what might happen next year. I have read the children's versions of *Romeo and Juliet*, *Julius Caesar*, and *Macbeth* to her and she sits and weighs the pros and cons for the class taking it on. This one is too scary or not enough characters for all the class members, or too much fighting ... —PARENT

William Blake's 1786 watercolour and graphite illustration of Oberon, Titania, and Puck with Fairies Dancing.

Heathcote and Bolton (1995) and other drama educators (O'Neill 1995; O'Toole 1992) have written about the te cher taking on a role that is not necessarily the most central or powerful in a drama. Having the teacher play Quince, one of the lowly workers within the play, allows her [the teacher] to be one of the players, not a king or queen who exudes power and privilege. In the earlier lessons, the teacher was often in a position to role play particular roles, Dr. Shaker's niece, for instance, and like the students, [that activity] became a place to warm up, practise various roles prior to doing the play. It is an important consideration to have the teacher continue role-playing with her students, by taking on a role in the production. This role-taking allows for a continuation of the class dynamics that were established, where the teacher is improvising, creating alongside her students. In the playing, a *status* and a *language register* change (Piazzoli 2012) occurs for the teacher, which includes the subversion of the teacher-student hierarchy and the kinds of language exchanges between teacher and student. As such, classroom patterns and interactions are disrupted during the playing, allowing students to see their *teacher* as a co-creator versus the person in charge. The teacher continues to be the responsible adult in the classroom, but a dynamic shift occurs in the learning as student and teacher work together, in tandem, to resolve the mysteries of the play in their preparation to perform the work for others. —RESEARCHER/OBSERVER

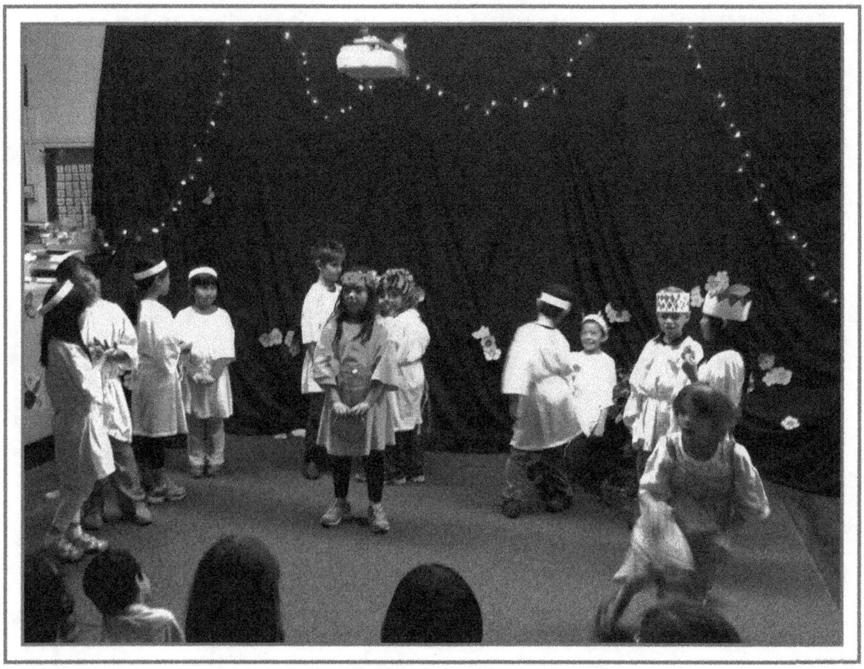

PART V

ADAPTED SCRIPT: *A MIDSUMMER NIGHT'S DREAM*

NOTE: The 30-minute adapted play script of *A Midsummer Night's Dream* that follows is available in class sets for student use. The font size in the student script version is large for easy reading. Please contact pep.sales@ubc.ca for ordering information or visit the publisher's website (www.pacificedpress.ca).

ACT 1, SCENE 1

Athens. The palace.

THESEUS *enters with* HIPPOLYTA *and* ATTENDANTS
Now, fair Hippolyta, our nuptial hour draws on apace;
Four happy days bring in another moon.

HIPPOLYTA
Four days will quickly steep themselves in night;
Four nights will quickly dream away the time.

EGEUS *enters with* HERMIA, LYSANDER, *and* DEMETRIUS
Happy be Theseus, our renowned duke!

THESEUS
Good Egeus: what's the news?

EGEUS

Full of vexation come I, against my daughter Hermia.

Stand forth, Demetrius.

My noble lord, this man hath my consent to marry her.

Stand forth, Lysander.

This man hath bewitch'd the bosom of my child.

I beg the ancient law of Athens.

THESEUS

What say you, Hermia?

Demetrius is a worthy gentleman.

HERMIA

So is Lysander.

THESEUS

In himself he is; but in this kind, wanting your father's voice,

The other must be held the worthier.

HERMIA

I do entreat your Grace to pardon me.

But I beseech that I may know the worst that may
befall me,

If I refuse to wed Demetrius.

THESEUS

Either to die the death or to become a nun.

HERMIA

So will I grow, so live, so die, my lord.

THESEUS

Take time to pause; and, by the next new moon,
Either prepare to die, become a nun, or wed Demetrius.

DEMETRIUS

Relent, sweet Hermia, and, Lysander, yield.

LYSANDER

You have her father's love, Demetrius; let you marry him.

EGEUS

Scornful Lysander!

LYSANDER

I am, my lord, as well derived as he,
As well possess'd; my love is more than his.
And Demetrius, he loved Helena,
And won her soul; and she dotes upon him.

THESEUS
I must confess that I have heard so much.
Demetrius, come, and Egeus.
Fair Hermia, look you fit your fancies to your father's will;
Or else the law of Athens yields you up—
To death, or to a vow of single life.

Exit ALL *but* LYSANDER *and* HERMIA

LYSANDER
The course of true love never did run smooth.

HERMIA
O cross!

LYSANDER
Hear me, Hermia. I have a widow aunt who hath no child:
And she respects me as her only son.
From Athens is her house remote seven leagues.
There, gentle Hermia, may I marry thee;
And to that place the sharp Athenian law
Cannot pursue us. If thou lovest me, then,
Steal forth thy father's house to-morrow night;
And in the wood, there will I meet thee.

HERMIA

My good Lysander! In that same place, to-morrow,
I swear to meet with thee.

LYSANDER

Keep promise, love. Look, here comes Helena.

Enter HELENA

HERMIA

Fair Helena!

HELENA

Call you me fair? Demetrius loves your fair;
O, teach me how you look, and with what art
You sway the motion of Demetrius' heart.

HERMIA

I frown upon him, yet he loves me still.

HELENA

O that your frowns would teach my smiles such skill!

HERMIA

The more I hate, the more he follows me.

HELENA

The more I love, the more he hateth me.

HERMIA

Take comfort: he no more shall see my face;
Lysander and myself will fly this place.

LYSANDER

To-morrow night through Athens' gates have we devised to steal.

HERMIA

And in the wood, where often you and I did meet;
There my Lysander and myself shall flee. Farewell.

Exit HERMIA *and* LYSANDER

HELENA

How happy some can be!
Through Athens I am thought as fair as she.
But Demetrius thinks not so;
I will go tell him of fair Hermia's flight:
Then to the wood will we to-morrow night.
Exits

ACT 1, SCENE 2

Athens. QUINCE'S house.

QUINCE *enters with* SNUG, BOTTOM, FLUTE, SNOUT, *and* STARVELING
Is all our company here?

BOTTOM
You were best to call them generally, man by man,
According to the scrip.

QUINCE
Here is the scroll of every man's name, which is thought fit,
Through all Athens, to play before the Duke on his wedding-day.

BOTTOM
First, good Peter Quince, say what the play will be,
Then read the names of the actors.

QUINCE
Our play is, *The Most Lamentable Comedy
And Most Cruel Death of Pyramus and Thisby.*

BOTTOM

A very good piece of work, I assure you.
Now, good Peter Quince, call forth your actors by the scroll.

QUINCE

Answer as I call you. Nick Bottom, the weaver.

BOTTOM

Ready. Name what part I am for, and proceed.

QUINCE

You, Nick Bottom, are set down for Pyramus.

BOTTOM

What is Pyramus? A lover, or a tyrant?

QUINCE

A lover, that kills himself most gallant for love.

BOTTOM

That will ask some tears in the true performing of it:
If I do it well, I'll move storms!
"The raging rocks
And shivering shocks—"

QUINCE *interrupting*
Francis Flute, the bellows-mender.

FLUTE
Here, Peter Quince.

QUINCE
Flute, you must take Thisby on.

FLUTE
What is Thisby? A wandering knight?

QUINCE
It is the lady that Pyramus must love.

FLUTE
Nay, faith, let me not play a woman; I have a beard coming.

QUINCE
You shall play it in a mask, and you may speak as small as you will.

BOTTOM
I can hide my face, let me play Thisby too,
I'll speak in a monstrous little voice. "Thisby, Thisby!"

QUINCE

No, no! You must play Pyramus; and, Flute, you are Thisby.

BOTTOM

Well, proceed.

QUINCE

Robin Starveling, the tailor.

STARVELING

Here, Peter Quince.

QUINCE

Robin Starveling, you must play Thisby's mother.
Tom Snout, the tinker.

SNOUT

Here, Peter Quince.

QUINCE

You, Pyramus' father.
Snug, the joiner.

SNUG

Here, Peter Quince.

QUINCE

You, the lion's part.

SNUG

Have you the lion's part written? Pray you,
　give it me, for I am slow of study.

QUINCE

It is nothing but roaring.

BOTTOM

Let me play the lion too: I will roar,
That I will make the Duke say, "Let him roar again!"

QUINCE

And you would fright the ladies, and then they'd hang
　us all.

BOTTOM

Then I will roar as gently as any sucking dove.

QUINCE

You can play no part but Pyramus!
Masters, learn your parts by to-morrow night;
And meet me in the palace wood. There will we rehearse,
For if we meet in the city, our devices will be known.

BOTTOM

We will meet; and there we may rehearse most obscenely
    and courageously.

Take pains; be perfect: adieu.

Exit ALL

ACT 2, SCENE 1

A wood near Athens.

PUCK *enters with a* FAIRY

How now, spirit! Whither wander you?

FAIRY

"Over hill, over dale, through bush, through brier
Over park, over pale, through flood, through fire
I do wander everywhere, and serve the Fairy Queen."
She and all our elves come here anon.

PUCK

The King doth keep his revels here to-night:
Take heed the Queen come not within his sight;
For Oberon is passing fell and wrath,
Since your Queen did steal the servant boy!

FAIRY

Are you not Puck, that shrewd and knavish sprite?

PUCK

Thou speak'st aright; I am that merry wanderer of the night. But, room, Fairy! Here comes Oberon.

FAIRY

And here my Queen. Would that he were gone!

OBERON *enters from one side;* TITANIA *enters with* FAIRIES *on other side*

OBERON

Ill met by moonlight, proud Titania.

TITANIA

What, jealous Oberon! Fairies, skip hence:
I have forsworn his company.

OBERON

Tarry, rash wanton: am not I thy lord?

TITANIA

Then I must be thy lady.

OBERON

Why should Titania cross her Oberon?
I do but beg a little servant boy.

TITANIA

Set your heart at rest: The fairy land buys not the child of me.
His mother was a friend: But being mortal, she did die;
And for her sake do I rear him up. And I will not part with him!

OBERON

How long within this wood intend you stay?

TITANIA

Perchance till after Theseus' wedding-day.

OBERON

Give me that boy.

TITANIA

Not for thy fairy kingdom. Fairies, away!

Exits with her FAIRIES

OBERON

Well, go thy way: thou shalt not from this grove

Till I torment thee for this injury.

My gentle Puck, fetch me that flower;

The herb I shew'd thee once:

The juice of it on sleeping eye-lids laid

Will make man or woman madly dote

Upon the next live creature that it sees.

PUCK

I'll put a girdle round about the earth in forty minutes. *(Exits)*

OBERON

Having once this juice,

I'll watch Titania where she is asleep,

And drop the liquor of it in her eyes.

The next thing then she waking looks upon,

(Be it on lion, bear, or wolf, or bull)

She shall pursue it with the soul of love:

Then, I'll make her render up the boy to me.

Enter DEMETRIUS *with* HELENA *following*

But who comes here? I will overhear their conference.

DEMETRIUS

I love thee not, therefore pursue me not.

Where is Lysander and fair Hermia?

Thou told'st me they were stolen unto this wood.

HELENA

Take my hand, good Demetrius!

DEMETRIUS

Do I speak you fair? Or, rather, do I not in plainest truth

Tell you, I do not, nor I cannot love you?

HELENA

And even for that I love you the more.

DEMETRIUS

I'll run from thee. *(Exits)*

HELENA

I'll follow thee and make a heaven of hell,

To die upon the hand I love so well. *(Exits)*

OBERON

Fare thee well, nymph:

Ere he do leave this grove,

He shall seek thy love. *(Re-enter* PUCK*)*

Welcome, wanderer. Hast thou the flower?

PUCK

Ay, there it is.

OBERON

I pray thee, give it me.
I know a bank where the wild thyme blows,
Where oxlips and the nodding violet grows,
There sleeps Titania, where I'll streak her eyes.
And make her full of hateful fantasies.
Take thou some of it, gentle Puck.
A sweet Athenian lady is in love
With a disdainful youth: anoint his eyes;
But do it when the next thing he espies
May be the lady: thou shalt know the man
By the Athenian garments he hath on.

PUCK

Fear not, my lord, your servant shall do so. *(Both exit)*

ACT 2, SCENE 2

Another part of the wood.

TITANIA *enters with* FAIRIES
Come, now a roundel and a fairy song.

FAIRIES *including* PEASEBLOSSOM, COBWEB, MOTH,
   and MUSTARDSEED *sing*

You spotted snakes with double tongue,
Thorny hedgehogs, be not seen;
Newts and blind-worms, do no wrong,
Come not near our fairy queen.

FAIRY
Hence, away! Now all is well.
Exit FAIRIES; TITANIA *sleeps*

OBERON *enters and squeezes the flower on*
   TITANIA's *eyelids*

What thou seest when thou dost wake,
Do it for thy true-love take. *(Exits)*

LYSANDER *enters with* HERMIA
Fair Hermia, you faint with wandering in the wood;
Our way is lost; let us rest if you think it good.

HERMIA
Be it so, Lysander: find you out a bed;
For I upon this bank will rest my head. *(They sleep)*

PUCK *enters*

Through the forest have I gone,
But Athenian found I none. Lo! Who is here?
Weeds of Athens they both do wear:
Sleeping sound, on the dank and dirty ground.
"Upon thy eyes I throw all the power this charm doth owe."
   (*Exits*)

HELENA *enters running behind* DEMETRIUS
Sweet Demetrius.

DEMETRIUS
Do not haunt me thus. (*Exits*)

HELENA
Happy is Hermia, wheresoe'er she lies;
For she hath blessed and attractive eyes.
But who is here? Lysander!
(HELENA *sees* LYSANDER, *but not* HERMIA)
Dead? or asleep? I see no blood.
Lysander, if you live, good sir, awake.

LYSANDER *awaking*
And run through fire I will for thy sweet sake.

HELENA

Do not say so, Lysander; Hermia loves you still.

LYSANDER

It's not Hermia but Helena I love:
Who will not change a raven for a dove?

HELENA

Wherefore was I to this keen mockery born? *(Exits)*

LYSANDER

Hermia, sleep thou there: And never come Lysander near!
Exits, chasing HELENA

HERMIA *awaking*

Ay me, what a dream was here!
Lysander, look how I do quake with fear:
Methought a serpent eat my heart away.
Lysander! What, out of hearing? gone? *(Exits)*

ACT 3, SCENE 1

The wood.

BOTTOM *enters with* QUINCE, SNUG, FLUTE, SNOUT, *and* STARVELING
Are we all met?

QUINCE

Here's a marvellous convenient place for our rehearsal. This green plot shall be our stage.

BOTTOM

Peter Quince?

QUINCE

What sayest thou, bully Bottom?

BOTTOM

There are things in *Pyramus and Thisby* that will never please.
First, Pyramus must draw a sword to kill himself;
Which the ladies cannot abide. How answer you that?

STARVELING

I believe we must leave the killing out.

BOTTOM

Not a whit: I have a device to make all well.
Write me a prologue; and let the prologue seem to say,
We will do no harm with our swords,
And that Pyramus is not killed indeed;
And, tell them that I am not Pyramus, but Bottom the weaver:
This will put them out of fear.

QUINCE

We will have such a prologue.

SNOUT

Will not the ladies be afeard of the lion?

STARVELING

I fear it, I promise you.

BOTTOM

Masters, to bring in a lion among ladies, is a most
   dreadful thing.

SNOUT

Therefore another prologue must tell he is not a lion.

BOTTOM

Nay, you must name his name, and half his face must be
   seen and you will say plainly: I am Snug the joiner.

QUINCE

Well, it shall be so. But there is two hard things;
That is, to bring the moonlight inside; for, you know,
   Pyramus and Thisby meet by moonlight.

BOTTOM

How do we show moonlight?

QUINCE

One must come in holding a lantern,

An' say he comes to represent the moon.

Then, there is another thing: we must have a wall,

For Pyramus and Thisby talk through the chink of a wall.

SNOUT

You can never bring in a wall. What say you, Bottom?

BOTTOM

Some man or other must present Wall:

And let him hold his fingers thus,

And through that cranny shall Pyramus and
   Thisby whisper.

QUINCE

If that may be, then all is well.

Come, sit down, and rehearse your parts.

Pyramus, you begin: when you have spoken your speech,

Enter into that brake: and so every one according to his cue.

(PUCK *enters unseen*)

What hempen home-spuns have we here,

So near the cradle of the Fairy Queen?

What, a play! I'll be an auditor, an actor too, perhaps.

QUINCE
Speak, Pyramus. Thisby, stand forth.

BOTTOM *as* PYRAMUS
Thisby, the flowers of odious savours sweet,—

QUINCE
Odours, odours.

BOTTOM *as* PYRAMUS
—odours savours sweet:
So hath thy breath, my dearest Thisby dear.
But hark, a voice! Stay thou but here awhile
And by and by I will to thee appear. *(Exits)*

PUCK
A stranger Pyramus than e'er played here.

FLUTE
Must I speak now?

QUINCE
Ay, marry, you must!

FLUTE *as* THISBY

Most radiant Pyramus, most ... *(Forgets lines)*
As true as truest horse that yet would never tire,
I'll meet thee, Pyramus, at Ninny's tomb.

QUINCE

"Ninus' tomb," man: why, you must not speak that yet;
That you answer to Pyramus:
Pyramus enter: your cue is past; it is, "never tire."

FLUTE *as* THISBY

O,—As true as truest horse, that yet would never tire.

BOTTOM *as* PYRAMUS *enters with a donkey's head*
If I were fair, Thisby, I were only thine.

QUINCE

O monstrous! O strange! We are haunted.
Pray, masters! Fly, masters! Help!
Exit ALL *but* BOTTOM

BOTTOM

Why do they run away? This is a knavery of them to make me afeard.

SNOUT *re-enters*

O Bottom, thou art changed! What do I see on thee?

BOTTOM

What do you see?

QUINCE *re-enters*

Bless thee, Bottom! bless thee! Thou art translated.

BOTTOM

I see their knavery: this is to make fun of me;
But I will not stir from this place: I will walk up and
 down here,
And I will sing, that they shall hear I am not afraid. *(Sings)*
"The ousel bird so black of hue,
The throstle with his note so true,—"

TITANIA *asleep nearby, now awakes*

What angel wakes me from my flowery bed?

BOTTOM *sings*

"The finch, the sparrow, and the lark,
Whose notes full many a man doth mark."

TITANIA

I pray thee, gentle mortal, sing again:
Mine ear is much enamour'd of thy note;
So is mine eye enthralled to thy shape;
On the first view to say, to swear, I love thee.

BOTTOM

Methinks, mistress, you should have little reason for that:
And to say the truth, reason and love keep little company
   now-a-days.

TITANIA

Thou art as wise as thou art beautiful.

BOTTOM

Not so, neither.

TITANIA

Out of this wood do not desire to go:
Thou shalt remain here, whether thou wilt or no.
And I do love thee: therefore, go with me;
I'll give thee fairies to attend on thee.
Peaseblossom! Cobweb! Moth! And Mustardseed!

FAIRIES *enter*

PEASEBLOSSOM
Ready.

COBWEB
And I.

MOTH
And I.

MUSTARDSEED
And I.

ALL FAIRIES
What's your will?

TITANIA
Be kind and courteous to this gentleman;
Feed him with apricots and dewberries,
With purple grapes, green figs, and mulberries.

COBWEB
Hail, mortal!

BOTTOM
I cry your worship's mercy, heartily: I beseech your worship's name.

COBWEB
Cobweb.

BOTTOM
I shall desire more acquaintance of you, good Master Cobweb.
Your name?

PEASEBLOSSOM
Peaseblossom.

BOTTOM
Good Master Peaseblossom!
And you?

MUSTARDSEED
Mustardseed.

BOTTOM
Good Master Mustardseed!

TITANIA
Come, wait upon him; lead him to my bower.

Exit ALL

ACT 3, SCENE 2

Another part of the wood.

OBERON *enters with Puck*
How now, mad spirit?

PUCK
Titania with a monster is in love.
While she was in her dull and sleeping hour,
A crew of patches met to rehearse a play
Intended for great Theseus' nuptial-day.
When the shallowest of that barren sort fled,
A donkey's nole I fixed upon his head.
Titania waked and instantly fell in love!

OBERON
This falls out better than I could devise.
But hast thou yet latch'd the Athenian's eyes?

PUCK
I did,—that is finish'd too,—

Enter HERMIA *and* DEMETRIUS

OBERON
Stand close: Is this the same Athenian?

PUCK

This is the woman, but not this the man.

DEMETRIUS

O, why rebuke you him that loves you so?

HERMIA

I fear thou hast slain Lysander in his sleep.

DEMETRIUS

I am not guilty of Lysander's blood;
Nor is he dead, for aught that I can tell.

HERMIA

I pray thee, tell me then that he is well.

DEMETRIUS

And if I could, what should I get therefore?

HERMIA

A privilege never to see me more. *(Exits)*

DEMETRIUS

There is no following her in this fierce vein:
Here therefore for a while I will remain. *(Lies down and sleeps)*

OBERON

What hast thou done? Thou hast mistaken quite
And laid the love-juice on some true-love's sight:
About the wood, Helena look thou find, bring her here.
I'll charm his eyes against she do appear.

PUCK

I go, I go; look how I go. *(Exits)*

OBERON *anoints* DEMETRIUS' *eyes*

Flower of this purple dye; hit with Cupid's archery,
Sink in apple of his eye. Wakest when she be by.

PUCK *returns*

Captain of our fairy band, Helena is here at hand;
And the youth, mistook by me.
Lord, what fools these mortals be!

OBERON

Stand aside: the noise they make
Will cause Demetrius to awake.

LYSANDER *enters with* HELENA

Why should you think that I should woo in scorn?

HELENA

You do advance your cunning more and more.
These vows are Hermia's: will you give her o'er?

LYSANDER

I had no judgment when to her I swore.

HELENA

Nor none, in my mind, now you give her o'er.

LYSANDER

Demetrius loves her, and he loves not you.

DEMETRIUS *awaking*

O Helena, goddess, nymph, divine!
To what, my love, shall I compare thee?

HELENA

O spite! I see you all are bent to set against me:
If you were men, as men you are in show,
You would not use a gentle lady so!

LYSANDER

You are unkind, Demetrius; be not so;
For you love Hermia; this you know I know.
With all good will, let me have Helena,
Whom I do love and will do till my death.

HELENA

Never did mockers waste more idle breath.

DEMETRIUS

Lysander, keep thy Hermia; I will none:
If e'er I loved her, all that love is gone.
Look, yonder is thy dear.

HERMIA *enters*

Mine ear, Lysander, brought me to thy sound,
But why unkindly didst thou leave me so?

LYSANDER

Why should he stay, whom love doth press to go?

HERMIA

What love could press Lysander from my side?

LYSANDER

Lysander's love for Fair Helena.

HERMIA

You speak not as you think: it cannot be.

HELENA

Injurious Hermia! Most ungrateful maid!
Have you conspired against me?

HERMIA
I scorn you not: it seems that you scorn me.

HELENA
Have you not set Lysander,
To follow me and praise my eyes and face?
And made your other love, Demetrius,
Call me goddess, nymph, divine, and rare?

HERMIA
I understand not what you mean by this.

HELENA
Fare ye well.

LYSANDER
Stay, gentle Helena.

HERMIA
Sweet, do not scorn her so.

DEMETRIUS *to* **HELENA**
I say I love thee more than he can do.

LYSANDER
If thou say so, withdraw, and prove it too.

HERMIA

Lysander, whereto tends all this?

LYSANDER

Hang off, thou cat, thou burr! Vile thing!

HERMIA

Why are you grown so rude?

LYSANDER

Be certain, nothing truer; 'tis no jest.
That I do hate thee, and love Helena.

HERMIA *angrily towards* HELENA

You canker-blossom! You thief of love!
What, have you come by night
And stolen my love's heart from him?

HELENA

Have you no modesty, no maiden shame?
Fie, fie! You counterfeit, you puppet, you!

HERMIA

Puppet? Why so? Thou painted maypole!
I am not yet so low that my nails can reach unto thine eyes.

HELENA *to* DEMETRIUS *and* LYSANDER
I pray you, though you mock me, gentlemen,
Let her not hurt me.

LYSANDER/DEMETRIUS
Be not afraid; she shall not harm thee, Helena.

LYSANDER *to* DEMETRIUS
Get you gone, or follow, if thou darest, to fight for Helena.

DEMETRIUS
Follow? Nay, I'll go with thee, cheek by jowl.
Exits with LYSANDER

HELENA
I will not trust you, nor longer stay.
My legs are longer to run away. *(Exits)*

HERMIA
I am amazed, and know not what to say. *(Leaves in pursuit)*

OBERON
This is thy negligence!

PUCK

Believe me, king of shadows, I mistook.

Did not you tell me I should know the man

By the Athenian garment he had on?

OBERON

Thou see'st these lovers seek a place to fight:

Hie therefore, Puck, overcast the night;

And lead these testy rivals so astray

As no one come within another's way.

With overwhelming sleep they'll lie,

Then crush this herb into Lysander's eye.

I'll to my Queen and beg her servant boy;

And then will I, her charmed eye release

From monster's view, and all things shall be peace.

PUCK

My fairy lord, this will be done with haste!

(OBERON *leaves*)

Up and down, up and down,

I will lead them up and down.

Here comes one.

PUCK *leads* LYSANDER *and* DEMETRIUS *and lays them down to sleep*

HELENA *then enters and immediately falls asleep*

PUCK

Yet but three? Come one more;
Two of both kinds make up four.

HERMIA *enters also; she lies down and sleeps*

PUCK

On the ground sleep sound:
I'll apply to your eye,
Gentle lover, remedy. *(Squeezing the juice on their eyes)*
When thou wakest, thou takest
True delight in the sight
Of thy former lady's eye:
Then all shall be well. *(Exits)*

ACT 4, SCENE 1

The same forest.

TITANIA *enters with* BOTTOM *and* FAIRIES; OBERON *is hidden*

TITANIA

Come, sit thee down upon this flowery bed,
Let me kiss thy fair large ears, and sleek smooth head.

BOTTOM

Where's Peaseblossom?

PEASEBLOSSOM

Ready.

BOTTOM

Scratch my head Peaseblossom. Where are Messieurs Mustardseed and Cobweb?

MUSTARDSEED/COBWEB

What's your will?

BOTTOM

Nothing, good messieurs, but to help Peaseblossom. I am marvellous hairy about the face, so I must scratch.

TITANIA

Say, sweet love, what thou desirest to eat.

BOTTOM

Methinks I have a great desire to have some hay: good, sweet hay.
Ah! I have a sudden need to sleep.

TITANIA

Sleep thou, and I will wind thee in my arms. Fairies, be gone.
(Exit FAIRIES*)*
O, how I love thee! How I dote on thee! *(They both sleep)*

OBERON *enters with* PUCK

Her dotage now I do begin to pity:
For, meeting her of late behind the wood,
I did ask of her servant child;
Which straight she gave me.
And now that I have the boy I will undo
This hateful imperfection of her eyes:
And, gentle Puck, take this mask
From off the head of this Athenian;
Make him think it was a dream.
But first I will release the Fairy Queen. *(Releasing the spell)*
Be as thou wast wont to be;
See as thou wast wont to see:
Now, my Titania; wake you.

TITANIA

My Oberon! What visions have I seen!
Methought I was enamour'd of a donkey.

OBERON

There lies your love.

TITANIA

How came these things to pass?

PUCK *takes off* BOTTOM's *donkey head*

When thou wakest, wake with thine own fool's eyes.

OBERON

Come, my queen, take hands with me.

TITANIA

Tell me how it came this night
That I sleeping here was found
With these mortals on the ground. *(Exits)*

*The lovers—*LYSANDER, DEMETRIUS, HERMIA, *and*
 HELENA*—are sleeping on the ground*

THESEUS *enters with the Court; sees the lovers*

But, soft! What nymphs are these?

EGEUS

My lord, this is my daughter here asleep;
And this, Lysander; this Demetrius is; and Helena.

THESEUS

Egeus, is not this the day that Hermia should give answer?

EGEUS

It is, my lord. *(Horn sound; the lovers wake)*

HIPPOLYTA

Good morrow, friends.

LYSANDER

Pardon, my lord.

THESEUS

I pray you all, stand. How comes this gentle concord in
 the woods.

LYSANDER

My lord, I shall reply amazedly,

Half sleep, half waking: but as yet, I swear,

I cannot truly say how I came here;

Our intent was to be gone from Athens.

EGEUS

Enough, enough, my lord; I beg the law!

DEMETRIUS

My lord, fair Helena told me of Hermia and Lysander's plan.

They devised an escape, and hither I follow'd.

But my love to Hermia melted as the snow,

The object and the pleasure of mine eye,
Is only Helena.

THESEUS
Fair lovers, you are fortunately met:
Of this discourse we more will hear anon.
These couples shall eternally be knit.

HIPPOLYTA
Away with us to Athens; three and three,
We'll hold a feast in great solemnity.
Exits with THESEUS, EGEUS

DEMETRIUS
Are you sure that we are awake?

HERMIA
It seems to me that yet we sleep.

HELENA
We dream.

LYSANDER
Let's follow. And along the way let us recount our dreams. *(Exit lovers)*

BOTTOM *awaking*

When my cue comes, call me, and I will answer:

My next line is, *"Most fair Pyramus."*

Heigh-ho! Peter Quince! Flute! What, they left me asleep?

I have had a most rare vision.

Methought I was, methought I had,

—Ah, man is but a patched fool.

I will get Peter Quince to write a ballad of this dream:

    It shall be called "Bottom's Dream." *(Exits)*

ACT 4, SCENE 2

Athens. QUINCE'S house.

QUINCE *enters with* FLUTE, SNUG, SNOUT, *and*
    STARVELING

Have you sent to Bottom's house? Is he come home yet?

STARVELING

He cannot be heard of.

FLUTE

If he come not, then the play is marred.

QUINCE

We have not a man in all Athens able to discharge
    Pyramus but he.

SNOUT

He hath simply the best wit of any handicraft man
   in Athens.

SNUG

Yea and the best person too.

BOTTOM *enters*

Where are these lads? Where are these hearts?

QUINCE

Bottom! O most courageous day! O most happy hour!

BOTTOM

Masters, I am to tell you wonders!

QUINCE

Let us hear, sweet Bottom.

BOTTOM

But not a word from me for now.
All that I will tell you is, that the Duke hath dined.
Every man look o'er his part; our play is preferred.
No more words: away! *(Exit* ALL*)*

ACT 5, SCENE 1

Athens. The palace of THESEUS.

HIPPOLYTA *enters with* THESEUS, PHILOSTRATE
'Tis strange my Theseus, what these lovers speak of.

THESEUS

More strange than true: I never may believe these
    antique fables.
Lovers and madmen have such seething brains.

HIPPOLYTA

All the story of the night told over,
Grows to something of great constancy.

THESEUS

Here come the lovers, full of joy. *(Enter lovers)*
Joy and fresh days of love accompany your hearts!

LYSANDER

Thank you, my lord.

THESEUS

Come now; what revels are in hand? Philostrate!
What entertainment have you for this evening?

PHILOSTRATE

There is a play your highness,
By hard-handed men that work in Athens.

THESEUS

Bring them in.

PHILOSTRATE

My noble lord, it is not for you.

THESEUS

We will hear the play.

QUINCE *enters nervously with actors*

If we offend, it is with our good will
That we come not to offend,
But to show our simple skill
That is the true beginning of our end.

SNOUT *as* **WALL**

In this same interlude it doth befall
That I, one Snout by name, present a wall;
Through which the lovers, Pyramus and Thisby,
   did whisper.
This be the cranny through which the lovers speak.

BOTTOM *as* PYRAMUS

O grim-look'd night! O night with hue so black!

O night, O night! alack, alack, alack,

And thou, O wall, O sweet, O lovely wall

Show me thy chink!

(WALL *holds up his fingers*)

Thanks, courteous wall:

But what see I? No Thisby do I see.

O wicked wall, cursed be thy stones for thus deceiving me!

FLUTE *as* THISBY *enters*

O wall, full often hast thou heard my moans,

For parting my fair Pyramus and me!

My cherry lips have often kiss'd thy stones,

Thy stones with lime and hair knit up in thee.

BOTTOM *as* PYRAMUS

I see a voice: now will I to the chink. Thisby!

FLUTE *as* THISBY

My love thou art, my love I think.

BOTTOM *as* PYRAMUS

O kiss me through the hole of this vile wall!

FLUTE *as* THISBY
I kiss the wall's hole, not your lips at all.

BOTTOM *as* PYRAMUS
Wilt thou at Ninny's tomb meet me straightway?

FLUTE *as* THISBY
I come without delay. *(Exits)*

SNOUT *as* WALL
Thus have I, Wall, my part discharged so;
And, being done, this Wall away doth go. *(Exits)*

SNUG *as* LION
You, ladies, you, whose gentle hearts do fear
The smallest monstrous mouse that creeps on floor,
May now, perchance, both quake and tremble here,
When lion rough in wildest rage doth roar.
But know that I, one Snug the joiner, am.

STARVELING *as* MOONSHINE
This lantern doth the horned moon present;
Myself the man in the moon do seem to be.
(Forgets his lines)
All that I have to say, is, the lantern is the moon and I,
The man in the moon; this thorn-bush, my thorn-bush.

FLUTE *as* **THISBY**
This is old Ninny's tomb. Where is my love?

SNUG *as* **LION** *roaring softly*
Oh—

THISBY *runs off;* **LION** *shakes* **THISBY**'s *mantle and exits*

BOTTOM *as* **PYRAMUS** *enters*
Sweet Moon, I thank thee for thy sunny beams;
Thy gracious, golden, glittering gleams.
But stay, O spite! What dreadful dole is here!
Eyes, do you see? How can it be?
Thy mantle good, What, stain'd with blood!
Lion vile hath here deflower'd my dear:
Which is—no, no—which was the fairest dame
That lived, that loved, that liked, that look'd.
Come, tears, confound; Out, sword.
(Stabs himself)
Thus die I, thus, thus, thus
Now am I dead, Now am I fled;
Tongue, lose thy light; Moon take thy flight:
Exit **STARVELING** *as* **MOONSHINE**
Now die, die, die, die, die. *(Dies)*

FLUTE *as* THISBY *enters*

Asleep, my love? What, dead, my dove?

O Pyramus, arise! Speak, speak. Quite dumb?

Dead, dead? These lips, this cherry nose, are gone:

Come, trusty sword; Come, blade:

(Stabs herself)

And, farewell, friends;

Thus Thisby ends:

Adieu, adieu, adieu. *(Dies)*

THESEUS

Moonshine and Lion are left to bury the dead.

DEMETRIUS

Ay, and Wall too.

BOTTOM

Will it please you to see the epilogue?

THESEUS

No epilogue, I pray you; for your play needs no

Excuse when the players are all dead. *(Polite applause)*

PUCK

If we shadows have offended,
Think but this, and all is mended
That you have but slumber'd here
While these visions did appear.
And this weak and idle theme,
No more yielding but a dream,
Gentles, do not reprehend:
If you pardon, we will mend:
Give me your hands, if we be friends,
And Puck shall restore amends.

APPENDIX A

GLOSSARY OF DRAMA GAMES AND STRATEGIES

THE FOLLOWING IS A GLOSSARY COMBINING GAME INSTRUCTIONS AND strategies in alphabetical order. A number of these activities and strategies are part of the common work of drama/theatre pedagogy with adaptations and alterations of activities introduced by various theatre/drama educators and practitioners.

- Character Walks
- Choric Voices
- Debriefing Circle
- Dress Rehearsal for Improvised Scenes
- Fill in the Space
- Flash-forward/Flashback
- Freeze
- Hot Seat
- Human Machine
- Interviewing in Role
- Mime or Physical Re-enactment
- Mirror Game
- One Back, Two Forward
- One Up/One Down
- Pass the Energy
- Play-building
- Salesperson
- Scarf Game
- Sculpting
- Soundscape
- Spotlight
- Status Game
- Stomp
- Tableau/Tableaux
- Tilt
- Visualization
- Voices in the Head
- Yes

Character Walks
Everyone walks around the room and follows brief instructions for how to walk: *limping, jumpy, slow, like you're 100 years old, like you're a baby.*

Choric Voices
Choric voice activities can be done with a full class or in small groups. They usually begin with a piece of scripted work offered to students. The goal is to bring the piece of literature to life through the voices of the group. Explore and experiment with a variety of tonal voice strategies—for example, slow down, speed up, whisper, speak louder, use cacophony, use one voice, use multiple voices—all in the effort to add colour and characterization to the text.

Debriefing Circle
A debriefing circle offers participants an opportunity to ask questions, reflect on the dramatic process, and reflect on their experiences. A debriefing circle should be held at the conclusion of a role drama and may be held after other drama activities and/or rehearsals. As facilitator, you might ask direct questions or guide the conversation by inviting each participant to speak about their experiences or to ask each other questions. To ensure that each student has the opportunity to speak, you might use a stone or another object to pass from one student to the next to signal that only that student may talk. The goal is to help students understand the dramatic process, to bring to the surface moments of learning, and to discuss choices (in actions or relationships) related to the drama process, their lives, and curricular inquiry.

Dress Rehearsal for Improvised Scenes
When students are preparing to present an improvised scene to others, a dress rehearsal is the last step before presentation. Giving students the opportunity to practise their scenes encourages them to work beyond simply brainstorming about what they plan to do and who is doing what role. Often, when students see their ideas enacted, new ideas come up, they develop new suggestions, and they make changes.

There are two ways of running a dress rehearsal. One is to have each group run through their scene with observers and/or the teacher giving suggestions and feedback. The second is to have the scenes rehearsed simultaneously in different locations in the room, without observation.

Fill in the Space
Walk around in a large open space "filling in" the space, trying not to have large openings. Call out a shape, such as a triangle, and ask participants to create that

shape to be seen from a bird's eye view. Other shapes can include letters (A, S, T, etc.) or numbers (8, 11, 3, etc.).

Flash-forward/Flashback

A flash-forward is an activity that encourages students to think about possible consequences of a situation, relationship, or choice of action. A flashback requires imagining what might have preceded and led to the present situation. A flash-forward or flashback can take the form of a tableau, an improvisation, or prepared scene. The challenge for participants is to incorporate their ideas about the present and future or past.

Freeze

This game does not need talking. However, you might first ask that participants do actions slowly, almost in slow motion, and exaggerate movements so that observers see possibilities. In a circle, two people begin an action—such as playing tennis. The players keep playing until someone in the circle yells "freeze" at which point they freeze. The person who stopped the action replaces one player and begins a new action, and so on.

Hot Seat

The hot seat usually involves an individual in role responding to questions from others, who may also be in role. The character in the "hot seat" might need to explain his or her actions, provide information, and so on, so the activity encourages critical and creative thinking about motivation, hidden agendas, moral character, and more. A hot seat activity could also have two or three individuals in role questioned by a whole group—for example, Titania and Oberon questioned about their quarrel over the human boy. Hot seats provide springboards to follow-up activities, such as writing in role.

Hot seat lessons can become heated, with questions and accusations flying fast and furious. The facilitator's role is to monitor the questioning and short-circuit any personal attacks or inappropriate questions. Generally, if the questioning might become intense, you might have two or three students share the hot seat as one character. They can then support, contradict, deflect questions to the other, and so on.

Human Machine

One at a time, enter the play space, each with one movement and one sound. (Movements should be controlled and relatively simple in order to sustain them for a long time.) Connect to one another to create a human machine. As the facilitator, you can vary the speed by asking the "machine" to speed up or slow down to increase or decrease productivity.

Interviewing in Role
Interviewing in role is a drama activity that provides information, allows questioners to probe deeply into the individual's motivations, and encourages critical and creative thinking. Interviews can be done in pairs or in small groups.

Mime or Physical Re-enactment
Mimed activities emphasize movement and gesture to demonstrate narrative development, ideas, or events. Instead of using dialogue, participants focus on movement and their bodies as means to communicate and express. For example, during the re-enactment inside Dr. Shaker's hotel room with Iago and his friends, students mime their understanding of the narrative. Students can experiment with silences, music, or other sounds to enrich mimed activities.

Mirror Game
In pairs, standing a few feet apart, one student is the leader and the other is the "mirror." The leader begins by making gentle, controlled movements, which are duplicated by the other student, as a mirror would. The goal is to mirror the partner perfectly, so the leader should move carefully and not try to trick their partner. After a minute or two, the students can switch leaders. Eye contact and focus are crucial.

One Back, Two Forward
In a circle, toss a ball from person to person—one person back (for example, to the left), two people forward (right). Keep going with that pattern, then add another ball, and then another one or switch the pattern.

One Up/One Down
In pairs, tell stories where each person tries to "one up" or better the other repeatedly. For example:

» *I feel great about the test: I think I may have got 80%.*
» *Oh yeah, I thought it was quite easy; I'm likely in the 90s.*
» *Well, given that there were bonus questions, I'm confident I got over 100%!*
» *Did I tell you I was just accepted at Harvard! ...*

Alternatively, tell stories in pairs where each person tries to worsen the story. For example:

- » *When I woke up, I couldn't move my foot. I could hardly walk.*
- » *Actually, when I woke up, my back was killing me. I had to drag myself on the floor.*
- » *Well, as I was telling you, my foot was sore and I could barely walk and I got to the stairs, where I slipped. Then I hurt my back and I hit my head ....*

Pass the Energy

In a circle, "pass the energy" around by sending and receiving a clap. Eye contact and concentration are crucial to passing the energy. You clap outwards, in the direction of a peer to send the energy, and clap inwards to receive the energy sent to you by this peer. The energy should be passed from peer to peer in a fluid fashion. You can begin by passing the energy around the circle to the person immediately beside you, but it should then move it across the circle. You can also play with the energy to make it come to life—for example, *it's hot, it can bounce, it can float.* A variation of this activity is in Part III, Lesson 2, warm-up activities (page 66), where the sender and receiver of the clap try to be in synchronization with their clapping.

Play-building

Play-building involves a process beginning with a stimulus of some sort (for example, a short piece of dialogue, a visual image, and/or a theme) and then groups working through a series of activities to generate an improvised piece. Here are suggested steps for play-building: (1) agree on the topic/focus, (2) brainstorm ideas on the topic, (3) possibly include characters, plot, setting, (4) generate an improvised script, (5) perform and reflect. The final piece is usually shared with others.

Salesperson

In pairs, take turns trying to sell the following items through a playful sales pitch: a three-legged horse, a blind donkey, a car with no wheels, a house with no roof.

Scarf Game

This is a game that does not need talking. Ideally, play the game in a circle. Leave the scarf in the middle and invite a volunteer to animate the scarf to make it represent whatever is wanted. For instance, the scarf can be manipulated to become a bowling ball with the help of your gestures and rolling up of the scarf into a ball. The scarf can become a beach towel, a large stirring spoon, a hairbrush ... It is best not to compel anyone to participate.

Sculpting

Sculpting is a drama activity for pairs in which one partner is the "sculptor" and the other, the "clay." Sculpting begins with establishing a trusting, respectful relationship between the participants. The activity itself requires one partner to shape/sculpt the other into a particular image or a series of images with slow, gentle manipulation; the partner being sculpted acts like "clay," moving his or her body in relation to the other partner's touch and/or instructions.

Soundscape

Creating a soundscape is a drama activity in which a group uses sounds (possibly including voices) to create a particular mood or environment or to provide insight into a particular character, situation, or event. The sounds can vary in tone, pattern, and volume to create a mood—for example, voices repeating particular words or sentences; sounds to evoke the wind, the squeaking of trees, and animals in the wood in *Dream*; abstract sounds to suggest a shopping mall.

Spotlight

Spotlight is a drama activity where small groups simultaneously do improvisations until you, as the facilitator, yell "spotlight!" and indicate one group with a flashlight or signal. At that point, the spotlighted group continues its improvising while all other groups stop their improvisation to observe and listen to the spotlighted group. When you signal that the spotlight is turned off, all groups can resume their improvisations. The goal is to allow greater numbers of students to participate in improvisations, share some of the ideas in them, and encourage critical listening and observation.

Status Game

This is a game that does not need talking. It explores high and low status. First walk around the room, all together, low to the ground. Then walk in some way higher—for example, with straight backs and arms extended. Continue with variations:

» walking with half a group in high status and the other half in low status, and then change
» in pairs at a bus stop with one chair—with one partner high status and the other low, and then change

Stomp

Standing in a circle, "send" the stomp around the circle by first lifting your left foot and then your right, and "pass" it along to the person beside you. You can vary the stomp: speed it up, stomp with your head up (not looking at your feet), stomp with eyes closed, or your own variations. When the group gets the feel and tempo of the activity, the stomping should almost sound like the human heartbeat.

Tableau/Tableaux

A tableau is a "frozen picture" consisting of individuals or groups using their bodies to physically illustrate a moment, decision, theme, concept, event, or idea. A series of frozen pictures (tableaux) could include a beginning image that "comes to life" briefly and then transforms into a final image. Variations include beginning with a spoken line, accompanying a tableau with sound and movement, and so on.

Tilt

Form two lines facing one another (best to be in semi-circle lines) and imagine a teacup on a saucer that is placed in the middle. Each person is standing on the edge of the saucer and does not want the teacup sitting in the middle to tip. Therefore opposite people must tilt, with the person across keeping the balance by either going forwards or backwards. This is similar to the mirror game, but instead of in pairs, an entire group tilts. As a variation, this could be done in a complete circle.

Visualization

Visualizations are activities in which students are invited to close their eyes and imagine themselves doing something in some other place—for example, taking a train trip, walking on the beach, discovering a locked trunk, hearing a knock on the door. Visualization is primarily a teacher-directed exercise and can start conversations, investigations, writing, and connections through metaphor, symbols, memory, and/or relationships.

Voices in the Head

This drama activity (which might also be called thought bubble or thought-tracking) involves verbalizing the inner thoughts and feelings of a person in role in a particular situation. It can be done in a variety of ways: for example, during an improvisation or tableau activity, each participant might say in role what he or she is thinking. Or observers could call out different suggestions for what the participants in role may be thinking.

Yes

In a circle, person A points to someone else in the circle—person B. Person A is asking for permission to take B's place. Person A can only move when B says "yes." B then points to someone else in the group—person C. When C says "yes," B can take C's place. C then points ... and so on.

APPENDIX B

MATERIALS FOR ROLE DRAMA 1: WHO ART THOU SHAKESPEARE?

Conference Poster

TEACHERS' ASSOCIATION 22ND ANNUAL CONFERENCE

DATE AND TIME: _____

LOCATION: _____ School

SPECIAL GUEST SPEAKER
Professor Pierce Shaker

READING FROM HIS UNPUBLISHED BOOK
The Story of Shakespeare

*Numerous lessons and workshops
offered by local teachers*

Special presentation by _____

APPENDIX B

Puck's final speech from *A Midsummer Night's Dream*

If we shadows have offended,
Think but this, and all is mended,
That you have but slumber'd here
While these visions did appear.
And this weak and idle theme,
No more yielding but a dream,
Gentles, do not reprehend:
If you pardon, we will mend:
Give me your hands, if we be friends
And Puck shall restore amends.

Postcard for Conference

INSTRUCTIONS: As you did for the poster, fill in the information for your school. Cut out the front and back of the postcard and make as many double-sided copies as there are students in your class. With stickers, colour code the postcards so that there are equal numbers of red, blue, green, black, purple, and yellow.

TEACHERS' ASSOCIATION
22ND ANNUAL CONFERENCE

DATE AND TIME: _____

LOCATION: _____ School

SPECIAL GUEST SPEAKER: Professor Pierce Shaker
READING FROM HIS UNPUBLISHED BOOK: **The Story of Shakespeare**

Special presentation by _____

APPENDIX B

Facts about Shakespeare

INSTRUCTIONS: Copy the pages with facts about Shakespeare. Then cut the copy into narrow strips (one fact per strip) and colour code the strips as indicated with stickers.

> Three facts you have discovered about Shakespeare:
>
> _____
>
> _____
>
> _____

[RED] *Shakespeare's early life and family*

- Shakespeare was born in April 1564 in Stratford-upon-Avon, England.
- He had seven brothers and sisters.
- His father John was an important member of the community.
- At age 18, Shakespeare married Anne Hathaway.
- He had three children, Susanna and the twins Hamnet and Judith.

[BLUE] *Shakespeare's language, plots, and plays*

- Shakespeare's plays use poetry and rhythm—not standard sentences.
- He invented or wrote first nearly 2000 English words—*bedroom, puking, unreal.*
- For his play plots, Shakespeare used many old stories people in his time knew.
- Shakespeare's word order is sometimes different than in English today.
- William Shakespeare is known to have written 39 plays.
- Shakespeare wrote comedies, tragedies, and histories.

[GREEN] *Shakespeare's comedies*

- Shakespeare wrote over a dozen comedies, including romantic and dark comedies.

- The comedies usually have a happy ending with several marriages.
- The comedies usually have young lovers overcoming challenges posed by elders.
- In the comedies, there are tricks and characters who are mixed up or disguised.
- In the comedies, friends or family get separated and finally find each other.

[BLACK] *Shakespeare's tragedies*

- Shakespeare wrote many tragedies—such as *Romeo and Juliet* and *Hamlet*.
- A tragedy's main character usually has a weakness, such as greed or ambition.
- The tragedies usually end with death and disorder.
- Tragedies have some comic relief—such as funny characters or scenes.
- Tragedies have characters who oppose or fight against the main character.

[PURPLE] *Shakespeare's Globe Theatre*

- The Globe was first built in 1598 along the Thames River in London.
- The Globe Theatre had three levels of seats circling an open-air stage and pit.
- In 1613, a cannon used in a play caused a fire that burned down the Globe.
- The Globe was rebuilt and opened in 1614, but then demolished in 1644.
- A new Globe was built in 1997 and still stands today, near the original site.

[YELLOW] *Shakespeare's influence and legacy*

- Shakespeare's plays have been translated into over 80 languages.
- Shakespeare's plays are *often* read and staged, even 400 years after he wrote them.
- Shakespeare's plays have been adapted in over 400 film or TV versions.
- Shakespeare is considered the best English writer of all time.
- Hundreds of cities hold Shakespeare Festivals every year where his plays are staged.

APPENDIX C
MATERIALS FOR ROLE DRAMA 2: ATHENIAN MARKET

Leaf Template

INSTRUCTIONS: Copy the leaf template onto coloured paper so that four to six colours are used equally, depending on the size of the class, to have one leaf per student.

APPENDIX C 195

Job List

1. **Abecedarian**—a teacher of the alphabet
2. **Actor**—a theatrical performer, someone who performs on stage for audiences
3. **Alchemist**—someone who studies or practises chemistry of the Middle Ages, including the goal of turning other metals into gold
4. **Ankle beater**—a young person who helps to drive the cattle to market
5. **Apothecary**—someone who prepares and sells medicines; pharmacist
6. **Back washer**—someone hired to clean wool or other fibres
7. **Backmann or Backster**—a baker
8. **Bagman**—someone who travels to sell goods
9. **Bellows-mender**—a person who fixes (and likely makes) the air bags used for musical organs or fires
10. **Binder**—a person who binds (ties or fastens) something, like parts of a book or grain into bunches
11. **Blacksmith**—a person who makes objects with iron, such as gates, tools, and weapons.
12. **Bookholder**—someone who prompts actors in the theatre
13. **Carpenter**—a person skilled in woodwork, who builds structures
14. **Cartographer**—a mapmaker
15. **Feller**—someone who cuts down trees so they fall, a woodcutter
16. **Flower girl or flower woman**—a girl or woman who sells flowers on the street
17. **Goldsmith**—a person who makes and sells items made with gold, such as rings, necklaces
18. **Joyner or Joiner**—someone who makes furniture or other woodwork
19. **Miller**—someone who works in or owns a grain mill (to grind grain) or other type of mill
20. **Pitman**—a person who digs pits, such as a common grave
21. **Pointer**—a person who sharpens needles or pins
22. **Potato badger**—a seller of potatoes
23. **Potter**—a maker or seller of pottery, earthenware
24. **Seedsman**—a planter or sower of seeds
25. **Tailor**—someone who makes or repairs clothing
26. **Tinker**—a person who travels about to fix kettles and cooking pans
27. **Weaver**—a person who makes cloth by lacing long threads, side to side and top to bottom
28. **Webster**—a woman who is a weaver

Scenes for Athenian Market Role Drama and Instructions

INSTRUCTIONS: Copy and cut into scenes so that each student will receive a copy of the assigned scene plus the group instruction.

GROUP A INSTRUCTIONS: Plan how one or two people will read the passage and the group will make a tableau, a "frozen" image, to present part or all of the text. It does not have to be a literal representation. Use your imagination to tell part of the story through your body.

> EGEUS: Happy be Theseus, our renowned duke!
> THESEUS: Good Egeus: what's the news?
> EGEUS: Full of vexation come I, against my daughter Hermia.
> Stand forth, Demetrius.
> My noble lord, this man hath my consent to marry her.
> Stand forth, Lysander.
> This man hath bewitch'd the bosom of my child.
> I beg the ancient law of Athens.

GROUP B INSTRUCTIONS: Plan how one or two people will read the passage and the group will make a tableau, a "frozen" image, to present part or all of the text. It does not have to be a literal representation. Use your imagination to tell part of the story through your body.

> OBERON: My gentle Puck, fetch me that flower;
> The herb I shew'd thee once:
> Having once this juice,
> I'll watch Titania where she is asleep,
> And drop the liquor of it in her eyes.
> The next thing then she waking looks upon,
> (Be it on lion, bear, or wolf, or bull)
> She shall pursue it with the soul of love:

GROUP C INSTRUCTIONS: Plan how one or two people will read the passage and the group will make a tableau, a "frozen" image, to present part or all of the text. It does not have to be a literal representation. Use your imagination to tell part of the story through your body.

> PUCK: Through the forest have I gone.
> But Athenian found I none. Lo! Who is here?
> Weeds of Athens they both do wear:
> Sleeping sound, on the dank and dirty ground.
> Upon thy eyes I throw all the power this charm doth owe.

GROUP D INSTRUCTIONS: Plan how one or two people will read the passage and the group will make a tableau, a "frozen" image, to present part or all of the text. It does not have to be a literal representation. Use your imagination to tell part of the story through your body.

> TITANIA *enters with* BOTTOM *and* FAIRIES. OBERON *is hidden*
> Come, sit thee down upon this flowery bed,
> Let me kiss thy fair large ears, and sleek smooth head.
> BOTTOM: Scratch my head Peaseblossom. Where are Messieurs Mustardseed and Cobweb?
> TITANIA: Sleep thou, and I will wind thee in my arms. Fairies, be gone.
> (*Exit* FAIRIES)
> O, how I love thee! How I dote on thee! *(They both sleep)*

GROUP E INSTRUCTIONS: Plan how one or two people will read the passage and the group will make a tableau, a "frozen" image, to present part or all of the text. It does not have to be a literal representation. Use your imagination to tell part of the story through your body.

> THESEUS *enters and sees the young Athenians asleep*
> But, soft! What nymphs are these?
> EGEUS: My lord, this is my daughter here asleep;
> And this, Lysander; this Demetrius is; and Helena.

GROUP F INSTRUCTIONS: Plan how one or two people will read the passage and the group will make a tableau, a "frozen" image, to present part or all of the text. It does not have to be a literal representation. Use your imagination to tell part of the story through your body.

> BOTTOM as PYRAMUS
> *O grim-look'd night! O night with hue so black!*
> *O night, O night! alack, alack, alack,*
> *And thou, O wall, O sweet, O lovely wall,*
> *Show me thy chink!*
> WALL *holds up his fingers*
> Thanks, courteous wall:
> *But what see I? No Thisby do I see.*
> *O wicked wall, cursed be thy stones for thus deceiving me!*

APPENDIX D

MATERIALS FOR ROLE DRAMA 3: CHARACTER MASKS

Character Masks

INSTRUCTIONS: Make one copy for each student in the class—preferably on thicker paper (like bristol board) rather than thin paper. You may wish to cut out the oval or ask students to do so.

Dramatis Personae: A Midsummer Night's Dream

INSTRUCTIONS: Present this list to the entire class.

Theseus is the Duke of Athens and a kind ruler. He recently won the war against the Amazons and will soon marry the Amazon queen, Hippolyta.

Hippolyta is the beautiful, powerful Queen of the Amazons who will soon marry Theseus.

Egeus is an older man in Athens, knows Theseus, and is the protective father of Hermia.

Hermia is a young Athenian woman and the daughter of Egeus. She is in love with Lysander and refuses to marry Demetrius despite her father's wish.

Lysander is a young Athenian man. He loves Hermia and suffers difficulties in the forest.

Demetrius is a young Athenian man. At first, he loves Hermia but eventually finds his true love in Helena.

Helena is a young Athenian woman and close friend to Hermia. She loves Demetrius.

Philostrate is an aid to Theseus, and responsible for organizing the festivities for the upcoming wedding of Theseus and Hippolyta.

Peter **Quince** is a carpenter. He directs his fellow workers to rehearse a play he has written to present at the Duke's wedding.

Nick **Bottom** is a weaver and a know-it-all. He wants to play *all* the parts he can in Quince's play. He will play the lead character, Pyramus.

Francis **Flute** is the bellows-mender. He is a young man whose facial hair is beginning to grow. He will play Thisby, a tragic female role.

Tom **Snout** the tinker will play the father of Pyramus and a Wall in Quince's play.

Snug the joiner is a shy person, and is cast as the lion where all he needs to do is roar.

Starveling the tailor will play Thisby's mother and Moonshine in Quince's play.

Oberon is the proud King of the Fairies. He argues with Titania and casts a number of spells.

Titania is the beautiful Queen of the Fairies. She is followed by friendly fairies who are loyal to her.

Puck is a fairy, Oberon's servant, and someone who loves to play practical jokes in the forest.

Peaseblossom is a fairy who is loyal to Titania and who serves Bottom in the forest.

Cobweb is a fairy who is loyal to Titania and who serves Bottom in the forest.

Moth is a fairy who is loyal to Titania and who serves Bottom in the forest.

Mustardseed is a fairy who is loyal to Titania and who serves Bottom in the forest.

Other **Fairies** are Titania's main servants and they know about Oberon and Puck's tricks.

Three Worlds—Creating Tableaux

INSTRUCTIONS: Copy and cut apart the copies so that each group has one or more copy of its world.

A. FAIRY WORLD—squabbling over a child: *Oberon and Titania have an ongoing argument over who should care for a young human boy. Titania insists that the boy's mother was a friend of hers and so Titania should raise the child. Oberon likes the boy and jealously wants him as his servant. Titania refuses to part with the boy, and in frustration forbids Oberon's company altogether.*

B. WORKERS—rehearsing a play: *The workers are rehearsing a play. Led by their director, Quince, they will perform* The Most Lamentable Comedy, and Most Cruel Death of Pyramus and Thisby. *Bottom is supposed to play Pyramus, a man who kills himself for love. Flute will reluctantly play Thisby, the lady Pyramus must love. Starveling will undertake the role of Thisby's mother, while Snout plays Pyramus' father. Snug, despite his shyness, will play Lion, who only needs to roar.*

C. ATHENS COURT—hosting a wedding: *Three couples have just been married— Duke Theseus and Queen Hippolyta, Hermia and Lysander, and Helena and Demetrius. Their ceremony is over and they walk towards family and friends to celebrate. Egeus and Philostrate welcome them in the garden.*

APPENDIX E

DREAM: A STORY VERSION

MIGHTY LAW OF ATHENS AND RUNAWAY PLAN

Excitement is growing throughout Athens and its surroundings because, in four days, Duke Theseus will marry Queen Hippolyta. Inside the Duke's palace, attendants and servants are busily preparing for the celebration. However, the merriments are abruptly put aside when Egeus barges in to see the Duke. Egeus, an irate father, says: "Full of vexation come I, against my daughter Hermia." Egeus has promised her to marry Demetrius, the young Athenian, but Hermia is strong-willed and refuses. She wishes to marry Lysander instead. In a kind but firm manner, Duke Theseus reminds Hermia of the Athenian law that allows fathers to choose their daughters' husbands; if not, they must die or become nuns and so never marry.

Left with little choice, Hermia and Lysander devise an escape plan to a nearby village where Athenian law does not rule. First they will meet in a nearby wood at dusk, and then they will make their way together to the village. Prior to leaving Athens, Hermia confides in her best friend, Helena, telling her the plan. However, the problem is that Helena loves Demetrius and she wants desperately to win his love. Helena decides to tell Demetrius about the escape plan. She thinks Demetrius will want to pursue Hermia, and Helena plans to follow also. As night falls, one by one, the four young Athenians leave the safety of the city to enter the spirit-filled wood outside of Athens.

A PLAY FOR THESEUS' WEDDING DAY!

A group of local workers has gathered near Athens to rehearse a play in hopes of performing it at the upcoming wedding celebrations of the Duke. The play is *The Most Lamentable Comedy, and Most Cruel Death of Pyramus and Thisby*. Led by their director Peter Quince, a carpenter, the budding amateur actors begin casting the play. A weaver named Nick Bottom is the most bombastic of the group and is slated to play Pyramus, a lover who kills himself most gallant for love. Francis Flute the bellows-mender will reluctantly play Thisby, the lady Pyramus loves. Robin Starveling the tailor will play Thisby's mother; while Tom Snout the tinker must play Pyramus' father. Finally, Snug the joiner will play the ferocious Lion, who only needs to roar. Despite his shyness and worry about memorizing lines, he accepts his role.

The very confident Bottom tells Quince that he could undertake the parts of Thisby and Lion as well. Quince firmly responds that Bottom "can play no part but Pyramus!" With excitement and fear, the troupe of amateurs set out to memorize their lines from the scroll by tomorrow night, when they will rehearse in the wood near Athens.

TITANIA AND OBERON CLASH

Meanwhile, in another part of the wood, Oberon, King of the Fairies, and Titania, Queen of the Fairies, continue a quarrel over who should care for a young human boy. Titania insists that the boy's mother, who died in childbirth, was a friend: "And for her sake do I rear him up. And I will not part with him!" Oberon is jealous and wants the boy to be his servant. Titania refuses to part with the boy, and in frustration, forbids Oberon's company altogether. To seek revenge, Oberon directs his servant, Puck, to squeeze the juice of a special herb into Titania's eyes while she sleeps so that when she wakes, she will fall in love with the first thing she sees, whether it is a lion, bear, wolf, or bull "she shall pursue it with the soul of love!"

While plotting their trick on Titania, Puck and Oberon overhear two of the escaped Athenians, Demetrius and Helena. Helena is deeply in love with Demetrius, but he rudely refuses her. Oberon feels sad for Helena and tries to help the pair. He commands Puck to anoint the young man (Demetrius) with a love potion when he is asleep so that Demetrius will instantly fall in love with the first person he sees when he awakes—Helena!

SPELLS EVERYWHERE IN THE WOOD

After Titania is lulled to sleep with songs by her fairies, Oberon mischievously sneaks in and pours the love juice on the sleeping Queen's eyelids. When she wakes she will fall madly in love with the first thing she sees.

Nearby in the wood, Lysander and Hermia are exhausted from walking and so lie down and sleep. Puck comes upon them sleeping and believes the young Athenian (Lysander) to be the man Oberon had directed him to (Demetrius). As per Oberon's orders, Puck nimbly anoints the eyes of the man (Lysander) with love juice, so that he will fall in love with the next person he sees when he awakes.

Within moments, Demetrius and Helena enter the same part of the wood. Demetrius is rude and unloving to Helena. He continues, but Helena stops and sits, demoralized. Soon, Helena notices that immediately beside her is Lysander. Is he dead or asleep, she wonders, and quickly wakes him. With the new love juice in his eyes, Lysander instantly falls in love with Helena (rather than Hermia).

> HELENA: *Do not say so, Lysander; Hermia still loves you.*
> LYSANDER: *It's not Hermia but Helena I love:*
> *Who will not change a raven for a dove?*

Helena cannot understand Lysander's change of heart and thinks he's making fun of her. She runs away, with Lysander in pursuit, which leaves Hermia asleep. Soon Hermia wakes up, alone and distraught, wondering where Lysander has gone.

PUCK PLAYS IN DEVILISH WAYS

In another part of the wood, the amateur actors are busily rehearsing their play and trying to resolve some of the acting challenges. They decide that it would be best to explain to their audience that no one gets hurt in the play and the lion is not real. They also agree to have Starveling play the moon because the moon shines the night Pyramus and Thisby meet. Last, they decide to have Snout play a wall because Pyramus and Thisby talk through a chink in a wall. Finally, they can rehearse!

Puck observes these hempen home-spuns and thinks it would be quite fun to have Titania fall in love with Bottom. Using his magical powers, Puck leads Bottom into a clearing within the wood and changes his head to a donkey's head. Unaware of his new appearance, Bottom terrifies his fellow actors with his animal ears and nozzle. The others run away screaming, leaving Bottom, singing away with his donkey head. He approaches Titania's bower and wakens her. She instantly falls in love with his hoarse voice and long ears! He joins Queen Titania inside the bower and she commands her fairies to:

> *Feed him with apricots and dewberries,*
> *With purple grapes, green figs, and mulberries.*

The mismatched couple are as happy as can be, much to Puck's sneaky delight!

LOVERS' QUARREL

Puck is delighted with the prank on Titania (making her fall in love with a donkey) and tells Oberon about it. Oberon then asks Puck about the love potion for the Athenian. Just then, they see Hermia and Demetrius, so discover that Puck has put the love juice on the *wrong* young man. Angrily, Oberon insists that Puck fix this mistake: Puck is to find and bring Helena while Oberon anoints Demetrius' eyes as he sleeps so that he will wake to love Helena. Within moments, Oberon and Puck do their magic, and Demetrius now rightly loves Helena.

However, all is not well yet. Lysander is still under the effect of the love juice, so remains in love with Helena. A quarrel starts between the two men as they both fight in vain for Helena. While the men quarrel, the long-time friends Helena and Hermia engage in a fight of wit.

> HERMIA: *You canker-blossom! You thief of love!*
> *What, have you come by night*
> *And stolen my love's heart from him?*
> HELENA: *Have you no modesty, no maiden shame?*
> *Fie, fie! You counterfeit, you puppet, you!*
> HERMIA: *Puppet? Why so? How low am I, thou painted maypole!*

In Athens, both men loved Hermia, while Helena loved Demetrius. But now in the wood, through Puck and Oberon's trickeries, *both* men love Helena. Hermia is angry about losing Lysander's love. Feeling mocked, Helena is furious.

In a playful manner, Puck overcasts the night and leads the lovers in the various directions in the wood before making them all fall asleep. Once the young Athenians are asleep on the ground, Puck uses the love juice to make everything right. When they awake, Demetrius will love Helena, Lysander will love Hermia, and all will be well.

RELEASE OF SPELLS AND ALL IS WELL

Oberon and Puck quietly approach Titania's bower to observe the donkey-loving Queen. Feeling sorry for Titania, Oberon releases the spell from her and tells Puck to remove the donkey head from Bottom. Titania and Bottom, now relieved of their spells, wonder how these things came to pass. Was it a dream? Hand in hand, Oberon and Titania leave with a sense of having resolved their differences.

Nearby, Theseus, Hippolyta, and Egeus discover the young Athenians sleeping on the dirty ground. With horns and their voices, the royal couple and Egeus wake them from their slumber.

> THESEUS: *I pray you all, stand. How comes this gentle concord*
> *in the woods?*
> LYSANDER: *My lord, I shall reply amazedly,*
> *Half sleep, half waking: but as yet, I swear,*
> *I cannot truly say how I came here.*

Still furious, Egeus is determined to have his daughter Hermia obey his wishes and marry Demetrius. However, Demetrius now swears his love for Helena. Theseus overrules the law of Athens, so that "three and three, we'll hold a feast in great solemnity." There will be a triple wedding at the palace! On their walk out of the wood and back to Athens, the young lovers try to figure out what has happened. Was it a dream?

PLAY WITHIN THE PLAY ON THE WEDDING DAY

Released from his donkey head, Bottom returns to the group of actors, who are relieved and delighted to see him. "O most happy hour!" Quince exclaims. Not only is Bottom returned, but news has arrived that their play is preferred! They will perform *Pyramus and Thisby* for the Duke and Duchess on their wedding night.

In front of the joyful Athenians at the palace, the workers-turned-actors nervously perform their play. A number of mishaps take place during the show as the amateur actors—led by the over-acting, over-eager Bottom—do their best to please. And please they do! But, their tragedy turns out to be more of a comedy, with Wall, Moonshine, and Lion explaining their parts to the audience rather than performing. At the climax of the tragedy, when the star-crossed lovers Pyramus and Thisby take their lives, the audience is in tears. But these are tears of laughter rather than tears of sadness. The actors are thanked, but kindly asked to leave as their efforts are now done. Theseus and Hippolyta and the four young Athenians enjoyed the festivities and are now newly wed. To end the story, Puck invites us all to think of this play as a dream and to put our hands together, "if we be friends," and clap in appreciation.

APPENDIX F

MATERIALS FOR LESSON 7: YOUNG ATHENIANS' JOURNEY

INSTRUCTIONS: Photocopy and cut out strips for each group, or project the page for viewing.

ACT 1

Hermia likes Lysander and Helena; Hermia does not like Demetrius.

Helena likes Demetrius and Hermia.

Lysander likes Hermia.

Demetrius likes Hermia; Demetrius does not like Helena.

ACT 2

Demetrius likes Hermia; Demetrius does not like Helena.

Helena likes Demetrius and Hermia.

Hermia likes Lysander and Helena; Hermia does not like Demetrius.

Lysander likes Helena; Lysander does not like Hermia.

ACT 3

Demetrius likes Hermia; Demetrius does not like Helena and Lysander.

Hermia likes Lysander; Hermia does not like Demetrius and Helena.

Lysander likes Helena; Lysander does not like Hermia and Demetrius.

Helena likes Demetrius; Helena does not like Hermia and Lysander.

Demetrius likes Helena; Demetrius does not like Hermia.

ACT 4

Hermia likes Lysander.
Helena likes Demetrius.
Lysander likes Hermia.
Demetrius likes Helena.

APPENDIX G

MATERIALS FOR LESSON 8: HEARING THE TEXT ACTIVITY

INSTRUCTIONS: Print and cut out each individual line of text so that the numbering and lettering appear.

BOTTOM:

1. *Sweet Moon, I thank thee for thy sunny beams;*

2. *Thy gracious, golden, glittering gleams.*

3. *But stay, O spite! What dreadful dole is here!*

4. *Eyes, do you see? How can it be?*

5. *Thy mantle good, What, stain'd with blood!*

6. *Lion vile hath here deflower'd my dear:*

7. *Which is—no, no—which was the fairest dame*

8. *That lived, that loved, that liked, that look'd.*

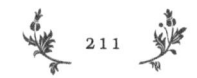

9. *Come, tears, confound; Out, sword, and wound*

10. *Thus die I, thus, thus, thus.*

11. *Now am I dead, Now am I fled;*

12. *Tongue, lose thy light; Moon take thy flight:*

13. *Now die, die, die, die, die.*

OBERON:

A. *I pray thee, give it me.*

B. *I know a bank where the wild thyme blows,*

C. *Where oxlips and the nodding violet grows,*

D. *There sleeps Titania. There I'll streak her eyes,*

E. *And make her full of hateful fantasies.*

F. *Take thou some of it, gentle Puck,*

G. *A sweet Athenian lady is in love*

H. *With a disdainful youth: anoint his eyes;*

I. *But do it when the next thing he espies*

J. *May be the lady: thou shalt know the man*

K. *By the Athenian garments he hath on.*

APPENDIX H

MATERIALS FOR REHEARSAL CONSIDERATIONS: CHARACTER JOURNAL

INSTRUCTIONS: Print a copy for each student or project these questions on the board.

1. What is your full name?
2. What else are you called? Do you have a nickname?
3. How old are you?
4. Where were you born?
5. When is your birthday?
6. What is your job or title? What kind of work do you do? What hours do you work? What conditions do you work in and for what income?
7. What about school: Are you a student now? How many years have you spent at school? What kind of schools are they? What are your marks? What are your favourite and least favourite subjects? What are your best and worst subjects?
8. What is your home life like? Describe who lives in your home.
9. Who is in your family—parents? sisters? brothers? How many older and how many younger brothers and sisters do you have?
10. What do you remember about the house you grew up in?
11. What do you do in your free time? What hobbies do you enjoy doing most?
12. Name and describe some of the games you played as a child.
13. What is your favourite childhood memory?
14. What is your worst childhood memory?
15. Who are your friends?
16. What do you think are your best and worst qualities?
17. What do you do for exercise?

REFERENCES

Ackroyd, Judith, and Jo Boulton. 2001. *Drama Lessons for Five to Eleven-year-olds.* London: David Fulton.

Ackroyd, Judith, Jonothan Neelands, Michael Supple, and Jo Trowsdale. 1998a. *Key Shakespeare 1: English and Drama Activities for Teaching Shakespeare to 10–14 Year Olds.* London: Hodder & Stoughton.

———. 1998b. *Key Shakespeare 2: English and Drama Activities for Teaching Shakespeare to 14–16 Year Olds.* London: Hodder & Stoughton.

Anderson, Michael. 2012. *MasterClass in Drama Education: Transforming Teaching and Learning.* London: Continuum.

Anderson, Michael, and Julie Dunn, eds. 2013. *How Drama Activates Learning: Contemporary Research and Practice.* London: Bloomsbury.

Baldwin, Patrice. 2008. *The Primary Drama Handbook.* London: Sage.

———. 2012 *With Drama in Mind: Real Learning in Imagined Worlds* (2nd ed.). London: Continuum.

Baldwin, Patrice, and Kate Fleming. 2003. *Teaching Literacy through Drama: Creative Approaches.* London: Routledge/Falmer.

Beare, David. 2011. "Social Art Effect: The A/r/tography and Complexity of Theatre Education Learning Systems, Developmental Stages, and Change Mechanisms." PhD diss., University of British Columbia.

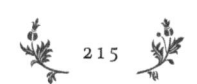

Beare, David, and George Belliveau. 2007. "Theatre for Positive Youth Development: A Model for Collaborative Play-Creating," *Applied Theatre Researcher* 7: 1–16.

Belliveau, George. 2009. "Elementary Students and Shakespeare: Inspiring Community and Learning." *International Journal of the Arts in Society* 4(2): 1–8.

——— 2012. "Shakespeare and Literacy: A Case Study in a Primary Classroom." *Journal of Social Sciences* 8(2): 170–176.

Belliveau, George, and Monica Prendergast. 2013. "Drama and Literature." In *How Drama Activates Learning: Contemporary Research and Practice,* edited by Michael Anderson and Julie Dunn, 277–90. London: Bloomsbury.

Boal, Augusto. 2002. *Games for Actors and Non-Actors.* London: Routledge.

Booth, David. 1986. *Games for Everyone: Explore the Dynamics of Movement, Communication, Problem Solving and Drama.* Markham, ON: Pembroke.

——— 2005. *Story Drama: Creating Stories through Role Playing, Improvising, and Reading Aloud.* Markham, ON: Pembroke.

Bowell, Pamela, and Brian Heap. 2005. "Drama on the Run: A Prelude to Mapping the Practice of Process Drama." *The Journal of Aesthetic Education* 39(4): 58–69.

———. 2001. *Planning Process Drama.* London: David Fulton.

Burdett, Lois. 1997. *A Midsummer Night's Dream for Kids.* Willowdale, ON: Firefly.

Campbell, Melvin, and JoAnn V. Cleland. 2003. *Readers Theatre in the Classroom: A Manual for Teachers of Children and Adults.* Lincoln, NB: iUniverse.

Carter, Richard. 2008. *A Midsummer Night's Dream: Original Verse Adaptation.* http://www.amazon.ca/Community-Shakespeare-Company-Edition-Midsummer/dp/0595483437

Catterall, James S. 2002. "The Arts and the Transfer of Learning." *Critical Links: Learning in the Arts and Student Academic and Social Development,* 151–157. http://www.curriculumsupport.education.nsw.gov.au/secondary/creativearts/assets/arts/pdf/citicallinksoverview.pdf

———1998. "Does Experience in the Arts Boost Academic Achievement? A Response to Eisner." *Art Education* 51(4): 6–11.

Clark, Jim, Warwick Dobson, Tony Goode, and Jonothan Neelands. 1997. *Lessons for the Living: Drama and the Integrated Curriculum.* Newmarket, ON: Mayfair Cornerstone.

Cramer, Neva, Evan T. Ortlieb, and Earl H. Cheek. 2007. "Multiple Ways of Knowing: A Theoretical Framework for Drama and Literacy in a Contemporary Curriculum." *The Reading Matrix* 7(3): 35–42.

Culham, Cameron. 2002. "Coping with Obstacles in Drama-based ESL Teaching: A Nonverbal Approach." In *Body and Language: Intercultural Learning through Drama,* edited by Gerd Bräuer, 95–112. Westport, CT: Ablex Publishing.

Curtis, Polly. 2008. "Teach Children Shakespeare at Four, Says RSC." *The Guardian.* March 3. Accessed February 10, 2014. http://www.guardian.co.uk/stage/2008/mar/03/rsc.schools

Deasy, Richard J. 2002. *Critical Links: Learning in the Arts and Student Academic and Social Development.* Arts Education Partnership, One Massachusetts Ave., NW, Suite 700, Washington, DC 20001-1431. http://www.gpo.gov/fdsys/pkg/ERIC-ED466413/pdf/ERIC-ED466413.pdf

Doona, John. 2012. *A Practical Guide to Shakespeare for the Primary School: 50 Lesson Plans Using Drama.* New York: Routledge.

Emmerich, Roland, director. 2011. *Anonymous* [film]. Los Angeles: Columbia Pictures.

Even, Susanne. 2011. Multiple Hot Seating. *SCENARIO: International Journal for Drama and Theatre in Foreign and Second Language Education* 5(2): 112–113. http://research.ucc.ie/scenario/2011/02/Even/12/en

Fels, Lynn, and George Belliveau. 2008. *Exploring Curriculum: Performative Inquiry, Role Drama, and Learning.* Vancouver, BC: Pacific Educational Press.

Gardner, Howard. 2000. *The Disciplined Mind.* New York: Penguin.

Heathcote, Dorothy, and Gavin Bolton. 1995. *Drama for Learning: Dorothy Heathcote's Mantle of the Expert Approach to Education.* Portsmouth, NH: Heinemann.

Hetland, Lois, and Ellie Winner. 2001. "The Arts and Academic Achievement: What the Evidence Shows." *Arts Education Policy Review* 102(5): 3–6.

Hulson, Maggie. 2006. *Schemes for Classroom Drama.* Stoke-on-Trent, UK: Trentham.

Kardash, Carol Anne M., and Lin Wright. 1987. "Does Creative Drama Benefit Elementary School Students: A Meta-Analysis." *Youth Theatre Journal* 1(3): 11–18.

Levy, Gavin. 2005. *112 Acting Games: A Comprehensive Workbook of Theatre Games for Developing Acting Skills.* Colorado Springs, CO: Meriwether Publishing.

MacKenzie, Donnard, George Belliveau, Jaime Beck, Graham Lea, and Amanda Wager. 2011. "*Naming the Shadows*: Theatre as Research." *Canadian Journal of Practice-based Research in Theatre* 3(1). http://cjprt.uwinnipeg.ca/index.php/cjprt/article/viewFile/29/18

Miller, Carole, and Juliana Saxton. 2004. *Into the Story: Language in Action through Drama.* Portsmouth, NH: Heinemann.

Moore, Blaine H., and Helen Caldwell. 1993. "Drama and Drawing for Narrative Writing in Primary Grades." *The Journal of Educational Research* 87(2): 100–110.

Neelands, Jonothan. 2004. *Beginning Drama 11–14* (2nd ed.). London: Routledge.

Neelands, Jonothan, and Tony Goode. 2000. *Structuring Drama Work: A Handbook of Available Forms in Theatre and Drama.* Cambridge: Cambridge University Press.

Novelly, Maria. 1985. *Theatre Games for Young Performers: Improvisation and Exercises for Developing Acting Skills.* Colorado Springs, CO: Meriwether Publishing.

O'Connor, Peter. 2010. *Creating Democratic Citizenship through Drama Education: The Writings of Jonothan Neelands.* London: Trentham.

O'Neill, Cecily. 1995. *Drama Worlds: A Framework for Process Drama.* Portsmouth, NH: Heinemann.

O'Neill Cecily, and Alan Lambert. 1982. *Drama Structures: A Practical Handbook for Teachers.* Portsmouth, NH: Heinemann.

O'Toole, John. 1992. *The Process of Drama: Negotiating Art and Meaning.* London: Routledge.

Piazzoli, Erika. 2012. "Engage or Entertain? The Nature of Teacher/Participant Collaboration in Process Drama for Additional Language Teaching." *SCENARIO: Journal for Drama and Theatre in Foreign and Second Language Education* 6(2): 28–46.

Pierce, Patricia. 2004. *The Great Shakespeare Fraud: The Strange, True Story of William-Henry Ireland.* Stroud: Sutton.

Polsky, Milton E. 1989. *Let's Improvise: Becoming Creative, Expressive and Spontaneous through Drama.* New York: University Press of America.

Poulsen, John. 2012. *Shakespeare for Readers' Theatre, Volume 1: Hamlet, Romeo and Juliet, Midsummer Night's Dream.* Neustadt, ON: Five Rivers Publishers.

Pura, Talia. 2002. *Stages: Creative Ideas for Teaching Drama.* Winnipeg: J. Gordon Shillingford Publishing.

Reason, Matthew. 2010. *The Young Audience: Exploring and Enhancing Children's Experience of Theatre.* Stoke-on-Trent, UK: Trentham Books.

Scher, Anna, and Charles Verrall. 1987. *Another 100+ Ideas for Drama.* Portsmouth, NH: Heinemann.

Shira, Ahava, and George Belliveau. 2012. "Discovering the Role(s) of a Drama Researcher: Outsider, Bystander, Mysterious Observer." *Youth Theatre Journal* 26(1): 73–87.

Siegel, Marjorie. 1995. "More Than Words: The Generative Power of Transmediation for Learning." *Canadian Journal of Education* 20(4): 1–12.

Sinclair, Christine, Neryl Jeanneret, and John O'Toole. 2012. *Education in the Arts.* Melbourne: Oxford.

Smith, Rob. 2012. "Drama in English." In *A Practical Guide to Teaching English in the Secondary School*, edited by Tim Green, 19–29. London: Routledge.

Smith, J. Lea, and J. Daniel Herring. 2001. *Dramatic Literacy: Using Drama and Literature to Teach Middle-level Content.* Portsmouth, NH: Heinemann.

Struthers, Joanna. 2005. "The Role of Drama." In *Teaching English: A Handbook for Primary and Secondary School Teachers*, edited by Andrew Goodwyn and Janson Branson, 71–89. New York: Routledge.

Swartz, Larry. 2002. *The New Dramathemes*. Markham, ON: Pembroke.

Swartz, Larry, and Debbie Nyman. 2010. *Drama Schemes, Themes and Dreams*. Markham, ON: Pembroke.

Tarlington, Carole, and Patrick Verriour. 1991. *Role Drama*. Markham, ON: Pembroke.

Theodorou, Michael. 1989. *Ideas That Work in Drama*. Cheltenham, UK: Thornes.

Wagner, Betty Jane, and Lisa A. Barnett. 1998. *Educational Drama and Language Arts: What Research Shows*. Portsmouth, NH: Heinemann.

Weltsek, Gustave. 2005. "Using Process to Deconstruct 'A Midsummer Night's Dream.'" *The English Journal* 95(1): 75–81.

Wilhelm, Jeffrey D. 2002. *Action Strategies for Deepening Comprehension*. Toronto: Scholastic Professional.

Winner, Ellie, Thalia R. Goldstein, and Stéphan Vincent-Lancrin. 2013. *Art for Art's Sake? The Impact of Arts Education*. Paris: Organization for Economic Co-operation and Development Publishing.

Winston, Joe, and Miles Tandy. 2012. *Beginning Shakespeare 4–11*. New York: Routledge.

Wolfman, Judy. 2004. *How and Why Stories for Readers Theatre*. Portsmouth, NH: Teacher Ideas Press.

Young, Chase, and Timothy Rasinski. 2009. "Implementing Readers Theatre as an Approach to Classroom Fluency Instruction." *The Reading Teacher* 63(1): 4–13.

INDEX

A
adapting goals/lessons, 13, 21
Anonymous (film), 31
artistic skills, 19
assessment
    for Athenian Market role drama, 46–47
    for Character Masks role drama, 53
    overview, 20, 39
    for Who Art Thou Shakespeare? role drama, 39–40
Athenian Market (role drama), 40–47

B
Beginning Shakespeare 4-11 (Winston and Tandy), 25
blocking, 107, 119–20
body, focus on, 116–17
body dominoes activity, 92–93
Bottom's speech, 100–101, 178
Burdett, Lois
    Shakespeare Can Be Fun!, 25

C
calendars
    sample production schedule, 108
    sample rehearsal schedule, 115
    sample three-month calendar, 23
    sample year-long calendar, 22
Carter, Richard, 25
casting, 108–9
character journal, 117
character list, 47–48
Character Masks (role drama), 47–54
character preparation, and drama activities, 75
character walks activity, 182
checking-in circle, 70
children
    confidence with Shakespeare, 102
    reasons for teaching Shakespeare to, 11–12
    See also students
choric voices, 109, 119, 182
classrooms
    as diverse learning environments, 13
    dynamics interrupted during role-playing, 124
    integrating drama into, 21–23
    as production space, 110–11
    resources for bringing Shakespeare into, 25
commedia dell'arte, 48
communication strategies, 19
costumes, 106, 111–12
creative thinking, 19
critical thinking, 19
cultural literacy, 11–12
curricular goals
    Athenian Market role drama and, 46
    Character Masks role drama and, 52
    drama activities and, 19–20, 23

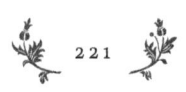

Who Art Thou Shakespeare? role drama and, 38

D

debriefing
    for Athenian Market role drama, 45–46
    for Character Masks role drama, 52
    circles, 20, 182
    importance of, 65
    during production, 122
    for Who Art Thou Shakespeare? role drama, 37–38
directing, 109, 121
Doona, John
    A Practical Guide to Shakespeare for the Primary School, 25
drama
    benefits of for children, 18–19, 19–20
    curricular goals and, 19–20
    goals of, 21
    reasons for teaching to children, 11–12
    teaching, 86
    See also Shakespearean plays
drama activities and games
    character preparation and, 75
    resources for, 24
    in year-long calendar, 22
drama education, 41
drama strategies
    resources for, 24
    role dramas and, 38
dramatis personae, 47–48
drawing, 20
Dream, see *Midsummer Night's Dream, A*
dress rehearsal for improvised scenes, 182

E

empathy, 19
ensemble, 40, 86, 91, 115, 116, 119
entrances, 120–21
exits, 120–21

F

fact-finding activity, 34–35
feedback, 121–22. *See also* debriefing
feeding in lines, 118–19
fill in the space activity, 66–67, 182–83
flash-forward/flashback activity, 183
Folger Institute, 25

freeze activity, 183

G

greeting game, 60
group activities, and shy students, 86
group movement activity, 84
groups and tableaux activity, 60–61, 71–72. *See also* shapes and numbers activity
group scenes, 119

H

Heathcote, Dorothy
    Mantle of the Expert approach, 40
hot seating activity, 39, 51–52, 64, 65, 183
    group, 73–74, 75
human machine activity, 183

I

"If we shadows have offended" (speech), 33, 180
improvisation, 29
interviewing in role activity, 184
"I pray thee, give it me" (speech), 100–101, 143–44
Ireland, William-Henry, 31

J

journal writing, 20, 70
    for character development, 117

L

language, Shakespeare's, 70, 96
"less is more" motto, 106–7
lessons
    Lovers' Quarrel, 87–91
    Mighty Law of Athens and Runaway Plan, 60–65
    overview, 58–59
    A Play for Theseus' Wedding Day, 66–70
    Play Within the Play on the Wedding Day, 97–102
    Puck Plays in Devilish Ways, 81–86
    Release of Spells and All Is Well, 92–96
    Spells Are Everywhere in the Wood, 76–80
    Titania and Oberon Clash, 71–75
letter writing, 20, 122–23
lighting, 111
literacy, 12, 18, 46
Lovers' Quarrel lesson, 87–91

M

magic potion, 51
Mantle of the Expert approach, 40
mask-making role drama, 47–54
memorization, 117–18
Midsummer Night's Dream, A
    Act 1, Scene 1, 128–33
    Act 1, Scene 2, 134–38
    Act 2, Scene 1, 139–44
    Act 2, Scene 2, 144–47
    Act 3, Scene 1, 147–56
    Act 3, Scene 2, 157–66
    Act 4, Scene 1, 166–72
    Act 4, Scene 2, 172–74
    Act 5, Scene 1, 174–80
    overview, 28
    reasons for focus on, 12
Midsummer Night's Dream for Kids, A (Burdett), 25
Mighty Law of Athens and Runaway Plan (lesson), 60–65
mime, 184
mirror game, 85, 184
modifying goals/lessons, 13, 21
moods activity, 76–77
music and sound effects, 111

N

newspaper, as play program, 113

O

Oberon's speeches
    "I pray thee, give it me," 100–101, 143–44
    "Well, go thy way," 118, 141
one back, two forward activity, 184
one up/one down activity, 184–85
ownership, by students, 40

P

paraphrasing, 117
parental involvement, 113–14
pass the energy activity, 66, 185
performance, *see* production
physical re-enactment, 184
planning, for drama integration, 21–23
play-building, 185
Play for Theseus' Wedding Day, A, (lesson), 66–70
Play Within the Play on the Wedding Day (lesson), 97–102
Practical Guide to Shakespeare for the Primary School, A (Doona), 25
problem solving, 19, 29
production
    as an event, 114
    goals of, 14, 21, 107
    and hot seating, 75
    "less is more" approach to, 106–7
    process, 107
    purpose of, 110
    sample schedule, 108
    spaces for, 110–11
program, play, 113
prompting, 118–19
props, 106, 112
Puck Plays in Devilish Ways (lesson), 81–86
Puck's speech, 33, 180
puppets on strings activity, 84

R

Readers' Theatre, 25
rehearsal, 114–15, 182
Release of Spells and All Is Well (lesson), 92–96
resources and references, 23–25, 30–31
retell narrative activity, *see* speaking wood activity
role dramas
    Athenian Market, 40–47
    Character Masks, 47–54
    overview, 28–29
    students in, 29
    teachers in, 29–30
    using, 30–31
    Who Art Thou Shakespeare?, 31–40
role-playing, 19, 29
Royal Shakespeare Company (RSC), 11, 25

S

salesperson activity, 185
scarf game, 79–80, 185
scene, definition of, 29
script, student version, 14–15. See also *Midsummer Night's Dream, A*
sculpting activity, 69, 70, 185–86
sets, 112
shake down activity, 97

Shakespeare, William, 28
   Who Art Thou Shakespeare? role drama, 31–40
Shakespearean plays
   confidence with, 102
   resources for, 24–25
Shakespeare Can Be Fun! (Burdett), 25
shapes and numbers activity, 67
skits, definition of, 29
sound effects and music, 111
soundscape activity, 87, 91, 186
spaces, for productions, 110–11
speaking wood activity, 89–90, 91
Spells Are Everywhere in the Wood (lesson), 76–80
spotlight activity, 186
spotlight on voice activity, 99–101
stage manager, 121
status game, 186
stomp activity, 186–87
storytelling activity, 33–34
students
   different types of learners, 13
   drama beneficial for, 18–19, 38
   engaged in drama, 59
   journey undertaken by, 123
   in role, 29
   shy, and group activities, 86
   See also children
suspension of disbelief, 80
"Sweet Moon, I thank thee for thy sunny beams" (speech), 100–101, 178

T

tableau/tableaux activity, 187
   collage, 94–95, 95–96
   See also groups and tableaux activity; sculpting activity

Tandy, Miles
   Beginning Shakespeare 4-11, 25
teachers, in role, 29–30, 109, 124
text work, 85
tilt activity, 187
Titania and Oberon Clash (lesson), 71–75
tongue twisters activity, 97, 116
transforming activity, 79, 80
transitions, 120–21
transitions activity, 76–77
transmediation, 40
transport activity, 79–80

V

visualization activity, 42–43, 187
vocabulary, teaching, 59, 62
voice
   exploring activity, 85
   spotlight on voice activity, 99–101
   vocal exercises, 116
   voices in the head activity, 187
volunteers, 113–14
Vortigern (drama), 31

W

"Well, go thy way" (speech), 118, 141
what are you doing? activity, 81–82, 86
Who Art Thou Shakespeare? (role drama), 31–40
Winston, Joe
   Beginning Shakespeare 4-11, 25
word wall, 59, 62, 63
worldliness, 11, 12
writing tasks, 20, 59, 70

Y

yes activity, 187
young learners, see students